P9-BJR-268

THE COURAGE TO FEEL

A Practical Guide to the Power and Freedom of Emotional Honesty

By Andrew Seubert

Illustrations and cover design by M. Rubin

Copyright © 2008 by Andrew Seubert

ISBN 0-7414-4707-X

Published by:

INFI∞ITY
PUBLISHING.COM
1094 New DeHaven Street, Suite 100
West Conshohocken, PA 19428-2713
Info@buybooksontheweb.com
www.buybooksontheweb.com
Toll-free (877) BUY BOOK
Local Phone (610) 941-9999
Fax (610) 941-9959

Printed in the United States of America

Printed on Recycled Paper

Published April 2009

Dedication

This first of my books is dedicated to my greatest teachers*:*

To the courageous clients whose stories fill these pages and who entrusted their hearts and souls to me in our work together;

To my son, Zane, for freeing me from a world of self-absorption through the indescribable gift of being a son's father;

To Clifford Smith, for mentoring me into manhood later in life with the experience of becoming a father's son;

To Erin, Jenna, Ariel, and Jocelyn, my stepdaughters, but really my daughters, for teaching me that love runs deeper than blood;

To my Beloved, Barbara, for loving me into more than I had ever imagined;

And above all, *to my mother, Lorraine*, for Life and for teaching me the enduring power of kindness.

Contents

Acknowledgments

I would first acknowledge all of the clients and family members who have courageously shared their hearts and souls with me, teaching me as we lived and worked together.

Names and identities have been changed for the sake of confidentiality, but the stories in this book, at times composites, reflect actual occurrences. Like any good myths, these anecdotes may not have occurred exactly as I describe them, but they are always true.

A great debt of gratitude goes to Cindy Barrilleaux, my editor from the start. Her insightful, yet sensitive, "blood letting" was critical in bringing this book to life and into form. Most importantly, her cheerleading frequently kept me in the game.

Thanks to Bill O'Hanlon for providing the workshop in which the idea for this book was conceived and for his ongoing support, and to Bill Phillips for encouragement and generous feedback at those early and confusing stages.

To Jack Walters and Fred Strugatz, co-directors of the IAM Counseling and Retreat Center in New Albany, PA, gratitude for the opportunity to create powerful workshops together and for their friendship and support as I learned my trade. A special thanks to Jack for introducing me to the idea that emotions carry messages with them.

A tip of the hat to the unknown scientist at Corning, Inc. who asked me to give him steps to aid him in learning about the emotional journey. As great questions do, his led to the heart of this book.

I would never have completed this project were it not for the encouragement and unconditional love of my family, particularly, my wife Barbara. No man is an island; they have taught me this well.

Finally, a grateful embrace for Cliff Smith, who has taught me so much through word as well as example, and for the Gestalt family that he has created and that I have been a part of for the past 15 years. In their presence, I have often wondered, "Why can't it always be this way?"

All of you are present in these pages. Thank you a thousand times over.

Foreword

Leigh McCullough Vaillant opens her now-classic textbook on psychotherapy for changing emotions and their defenses, *Changing Character,* with this statement on the centrality of emotions to mental health and to the art of living:

> The mechanism of emotional change is the most central issue in the mental health field . . . . It is emotional change that is necessary for healing the long-standing painfulness of character pathology. Yet emotional change is the least studied and most misunderstood area in the field.

She then quotes psychiatrist Robert G. Robinson, "It is primarily emotional change that lies at the heart of human suffering associated with mental disorders and constitutes much of our work in psychotherapy and pharmacotherapy." (Vaillant, Leigh McCullough. *Changing Character*, New York, NY: Basic Books, 1997)

If mental health professionals are still advancing their knowledge of emotional experience and emotional change, one can only imagine how little the typical person knows about the central, necessary and positive role that emotions play in becoming competent in the art of living.

After 40 years of conducting emotion-focused therapy with thousands of clients and training hundreds of therapists, I can finally recommend a user-friendly, simple, yet profound book to jumpstart the journey to emotional honesty, a competency that is at the heart of being fully human.

The Courage to Feel: A Practical Guide to the Power and Freedom of Emotional Honesty creatively presents a four-step process that teaches the reader "how to do" emotions. Andrew Seubert, a gifted psychotherapist and trainer, explains in a down-to-earth, intimate tone, what we need to know about our feelings, but were never taught. His book aims to change the crippling attitude that emotions are "pesky things to be controlled and managed" to an understanding of the reality that emotions are a powerful GPS system for negotiating life happily. Readers discover that developing emotional honesty can launch them on a journey of self-transformation that is challenging, exciting, and, if pursued with determination, guaranteed to free them from lives of heartache and frustration.

Andrew's enthusiastic conviction that we are capable of great inner change and lives of deep authenticity is based on decades of his helping clients do this very work. And his conviction is contagious.

This heartwarming and challenging book contains chapters on all aspects of making friends with our feelings, including the ways we deny, avoid, and wall off our feelings, and how we can listen to the messages of our feelings. It concludes with sections on living with emotional competence in marriage, family, love relationships, the workplace, and within society and the global community. Finally, the inherent relationship between emotional honesty and spiritual authenticity is explored. In every chapter, through a series of brief, emotionally engaging exercises, readers gain experiential learning. Vivid, anecdotal descriptions from counseling settings and situations of everyday life enhance this learning.

Interspersed throughout the book is Andrew's engaging fable of Simon the Turtle. This once-unhappy creature confined within his own shell goes on a journey with the help of his friend Ronald to a life of joy and freedom. The fable illustrates the workings of the four steps in living an emotionally honest and growth-oriented life.

I encourage readers not to be fooled by the tone of this book. Its aim is to simplify and to make available the understandings of the emotions found in the ever-growing scholarly writing in psychology and psychotherapy. The content and approach are never simplistic; rather they are profoundly simple. Such is the accomplishment of a talented teacher and writer.

The Courage to Feel not only inspires, but also empowers. It provides descriptions of emotional experiences and phenomena readers are likely to encounter as they strive to create rich and fulfilling lives. Readers from all walks of life can benefit from the pragmatic, step-by-step coaching and exercises on how to achieve emotional integrity. Moreover, counselors, therapists, and clients alike will profit from having a detailed blueprint for dealing with the emotional twists and turns of their journeys.

I hope this book finds it way into junior and senior high schools, colleges, graduate schools, churches, and the workplace, where emotional denial creates cultures of mistrust, inefficiency, and destructive behaviors. Hospitals, prisons, rehabilitation and addiction treatment centers will all benefit from the wisdom and instructional clarity of this book. I think it is likely to become a basic requirement in many training programs for helping professionals

This book is a tour de force. I don't know of anything in the literature that is such a comprehensive and clear guide to understanding the central role of emotions in living a healthy, "whole-some", and sacred life, enabling one to experience "the rapture of being alive." With *The Courage to Feel*, Andrew has done many a great service.

Clifford O. Smith, Ph.D.
Licensed Psychologist and Psychotherapist
Wilmington, Delaware

PART ONE

Why Bother?

Introduction

Leaving home is hard. It's hard to leave high school friends for college. It's hard to leave a family home for our own apartment on the other side of town. It's hard to choose a career that takes us far from our neighborhood. Many of us do these things anyway, believing we've made the break. We've grown up, so we're convinced. Yet no one told us that we might be thirty, forty or fifty-something and still unable to leave home.

No one told us that we could achieve work skills and academic degrees, marry and bring children into the world while suffering a handicap that could ruin it all. No one taught us that as long as we responded and reacted emotionally to the world around us as we had as children, leaving home would never happen.

Even after our physical separation has been achieved, we often continue to struggle with feelings, just as we had in our early years. In those younger days, rare was the adult or mentor who had developed emotional wings of his or her own, thereby making it impossible for us to take flight. They couldn't show us *how* to listen to our feelings, and very few could model the *courage* to feel. Most of them hadn't left home either.

I recall Deborah, a young, blond girl in the fifth grade in the mid-fifties, in a square, brick building that was St. Anselm's Catholic school in Brooklyn. She had been called in front of the class to show us how she signed her name. Not knowing what to expect, Deborah wrote her name, adding a curl to the last letter.

The nun's face took on a scowl, as her voice intensified: "Showing off again!" She grabbed an eraser, wiping away the curl and any sign of individuality from the blackboard. In that moment, Deborah learned to take out of her life any curls that might attract embarrassment and shame. She learned a lesson common to many of us.

What happened to Deborah happened to me as well. In so many situations, my mother had learned to ask, "What will people think?" It was a question driven by the fear of standing out, of being criticized, of being labeled as selfish. It wasn't until I was an adult that I realized that my mother's question had become my own and that it was holding me back. Unaware of and unable to face the fear and embarrassment associated with standing out, I was emotionally stuck at home.

The belief that one must never shine too much set off fear and shame, which stood as sentinels, keeping me from stepping outside the comfort zone of adult approval. No one ever told Deborah or me what to do with our feelings and why they were happening. Instead, we were ruled, rather than guided, by them. We grew older, doing anything to avoid setting those feelings off. We still lived at home emotionally, although a thousand miles away.

The Courage to Feel is about taking the emotional journey that leads us from the world of our childhood into an adult life of purpose and self-direction. It is a user's guide for tapping into the guidance and passion of our feelings.

As the years passed, I gained a sense that my emotions had positive purpose, as well as power. Yet, they needed to be released from their unconscious exile, from the way they had been buried alive. This freedom came through my most powerful lesson, which was still to come.

I was driving through an early morning, Pennsylvania mist on the way to the beginning of a three-year training for therapists. I rode with a colleague, Rose, more seasoned, more credentialed, and locally respected. I was the new kid on the block, still needing to prove myself, still believing I had to catch up or make up for something. No one ever taught me otherwise, particularly my father, who was rarely around.

"But, hey," I thought to myself, "I'm okay. I'm cool. I can learn things on my own." But something unfinished kept me from feeling completely convinced. I still didn't feel grown up, and I was almost forty.

Rose and I finally arrived at a century-old Pennsylvania lodge where our training was to take place. We entered the large meeting room filled with fourteen other therapists, a fire burning on that chilly morning.. The first person I noticed was the man who was about to change my life in ways I could not imagine.

Stretched out on the floor at the head of a circle of professionals, Cliff Smith smiled and invited us in. As he spoke, his words carried clarity, wisdom and kindness, and yet, at the end of the first weekend, I was telling him and the group, "I have a very hard time letting anyone teach me anything."

"That would be a good one to watch," he said, giving me all the room to figure this one out for myself.

On the fourth weekend, Cliff announced that he was inviting a body-centered Gestalt therapist to Wilmington, Delaware to give a two-day training. I signed up and joined 75 other therapists and psychologists, most of them trained or, at least influenced, by Cliff.

At the training, we were all seated in a large circle on the floor. To my surprise, Cliff made his way around the outside of the circle and sat in the small space next to me. He leaned over and said, "I really want you to understand what he's doing," and began to explain the non-verbal bodywork that was taking place in front of us. He was teaching me, just me, and I was soaking it in, letting myself be taught.

On Saturday evening I drove back with a few colleagues. As I thought of Cliff's attention to me in the circle, a feeling came up, one that had been buried since I was a kid. It broke loose and sobs erupted. It was such a strange, long forgotten sensation. The feelings were so strong I could barely breathe. It seemed like they could choke me.

"Let it go," my colleague who was driving encouraged. I did and simply let whatever it was tear loose. The tidal waves of emotion came and then went. I rode them. I was breathing again. I felt alive, actually more alive than I had ever felt. Recalling the time in the circle, I realized no one had ever taught me like that, particularly my father. I missed out on something as a kid, and, in feeling this loss fully, I finally realized that my father was not only gone, but had never been there. The paradox, however, was that as soon as I recognized and released those feelings, there was finally space inside to take in a father's presence. I was finally leaving home.

I had always wondered when I would grow up, when I would feel like an adult among men. The missing piece was having someone teach me, believe in me, and cheer me on. I needed to know what it felt like to be a father's son.

The gate that opened me to this moment was the power of honest emotion. I knew then that part of my own calling was to contribute to the emotional life of the world, to connect fathers and sons, parents and children, husbands and wives through emotional truth.

I began to recognize how many of my clients, friends and family were living only partial lives, just as I had, by keeping much of their vitality under emotional mufflers. I wanted to teach them how to embrace their emotional radar system, as I came to call it. There were books about emotions, but I wanted them to have something to read that was practical, something that would excite their desire to grow up emotionally.

And so *The Courage to Feel* was born. It is a gift of gratitude to the people who have entrusted their tender and intense emotions to me in the process of learning how to leave home at last. And to those whom I have not yet met, I offer this work in the hope that it will be a guide, a light to accompany you as you journey into the life you were born to live.

Chapter 1:

We Have Feelings Because…?

Many of us are handicapped without knowing it. We enter the race to go the distance only to realize that we've left one of our legs at the starting line. We wonder why we never finish, why the race seems so much harder than we expected or had hoped it would be.

We have survived as a species and travel through life because we have various ways of knowing, an advantage that has enabled us to outlive, overcome and, at times, abuse other forms of life. We gather information with our thinking mind, our body intuition, our creative intuition, and our emotional repertoire. To ignore any of these, particularly the mind or the emotions, is to run the race with one leg at best.

This book is meant to inspire and teach you how to become an expert about yourself, primarily your emotional system. Nothing less than that. In later chapters, I will be more specific as to how feelings work, what they do for us and what to do with them, since this is a "hands-on" book. For now I will focus on the barriers: the fears, the shame and, at times, the disdain many of us associate with a "show of feelings" and being "ruled by emotions." Despite the growing pool of information about the damage we suffer by neglecting our emotions, most people would rather ignore, deny, or surgically remove the pesky and painful things.

Courage is not a quality typically associated with emotions. Men, in particular, seem to be genetically and culturally damned when it comes to these "touchy feely" things that get in the way of getting a job done, relaxing on a fishing boat or tennis court, or hanging out with a spouse without having to talk or relate. One of the greatest stigmas men face is that it is soft, weak, and unmanly to feel, much less to show emotions. This attitude is deeply embedded in corporate and business cultures, precisely the places where men have to prove their worth on a daily basis.

Underneath the strutting and the peacocking, men are often afraid to feel. Unquestioned shame and perceived inadequacy drive them down endless corridors of work and career. Ignored sadness sets them up for callousness and depression. The fear of intimacy, of relational closeness beyond orgasm, leads to a loneliness and disconnection that are often buried in busyness and other addictions.

Brendan is an old friend, a prince among men, many would say. He's your classic nice guy. So nice that at times I'd like to piss him off just to see if anyone is home, to see if there's an edge and not just a butter knife. He wants so much to be good--rather, to be seen as good. A good boy. Above all else, he fears reprimand, disapproval, and is even more terrified of hurting someone else. Conflict is not his strong suit.

He learned all of this from his father, a businessman loved by all in their community, a small, rural town in upstate New York. His father would always be out there, in full plumage, greeting everyone, checking in on each person's health and home life. But he would bury his head in the sand at the first sign of disagreement. Brendan inherited this legacy, so much so that the very thought of disagreeing, of not receiving the championship ring of acceptance, would stir up a boiling pot of fear and shame.

He sits across from me now in my living room, amiable, agreeable, unable to tell me or his wife why he feels unconnected to most people, why he can't tell his children he loves them, or say he's angry when he is used and abused at work, or bring himself to attend the memorial service of a beloved, elderly woman he has known since childhood. Over the years, he has come to fear embarrassment, the guilt and shame of offending anyone, and the fear of fear itself. The inability to face these emotions and the beliefs that feed them keep Brendan from truly leaving home thirty years after departing from his parents' house for college.

These days he takes on the work of two, sometimes three people at the job since his company began to downsize. He's afraid to speak up about the overload and appear not up to the task, but hardly notices the fear and the sense of inadequacy, since he's either working without a pause or coming home and drinking to decompress. After the first of several evening drinks, he begins to crash, gets irritable and leaves the kids to "the wife." He heads to a separate room, numbing his frustrations with the television and one more vodka. If he were able to notice what his emotional guidance was telling him, his job and his home life would be quite different.

Conditioning and fear of feelings, however, are not limited to men, but are very much a part of how women deal with emotions as well. A woman may feel more (the genetic piece) and may express more (the conditioned piece), but the restrictions often come in the form of which feelings are tolerable. The fear of guilt, for example, can render a woman incapable of taking care of herself. The fear of feeling or showing anger can turn her into a doormat.

Brendan's wife, Gail, works outside the home, and then picks up their two children from after-school care. She received her emotional training by osmosis from her mother who orbited around her father's workaholism and angry depression. On a typical day, tired herself, she sees Brendan walk through the front door with nothing left for her or the kids. She watches the vodka disappear from the bottle and a dark cloud settle over her husband's head.

"How was your day?" she ventures.

"The same as always. Same old shit..."

"Want to talk about it?"

"What the hell good is that going to do?" he asks, the irritability rising. His wife is becoming a target for his anger to hang on.

Through all of this, a stockpile of emotion is building inside of Gail. There is anger of her own, hurt, loneliness, very little of which she allows herself to notice, much in the tradition of her mother. Most of the time, she cries quietly when the children aren't looking and after Brendan has left the room.

Months later, Brendan visits me again.

"I don't get it!" he tells me. "She just, out of the clear blue, tells me she's wanting a divorce."

"Did she ever talk to you about why she was unhappy?"

"She says she did, but I don't remember anything like that. I just think she's losing it."

In my private practice, I have heard this story so many times. The pressures of contemporary life, particularly with both adults in a family needing to work, create personal depletion and interpersonal distance. The emotions that might have served as warning signals and motivators for balanced change are ignored, denied, and buried. The eventual price is painfully high.

These quandaries usually have their origins earlier in life, where we are first thrust into relationships with family and, later, with teachers, schoolmates and report cards. We and our children enter the world with its maze of events and storm of cultural influences without being taught how to use our innate compass, the guidance of the emotional radar with which we were born. Children teased repeatedly withdraw into depression or assault, not knowing how to recognize, tolerate and deal with the emotional signals that arise. Like a slap across the face, shame is, as author Jodi Picoult writes, a "five-fingered word" that easily catalyzes depression, anxiety, or their opposite, aggression. Our youth have become greater and greater consumers of mood medication and perpetrators of shooting sprees.

Cynthia is a talented, attractive fourteen-year-old, adopted shortly after birth. She has more of a muscular physique than a model's stick figure. Her biological father appeared at her home when she was seven. Drunk and insisting that he be able to take his daughter back, he was, instead, taken away by the police. Not long after, her adoptive father left home with their twenty-something babysitter. Where are Ozzie and Harriet when you need them?

Cynthia learned very early in life not to feel. It was simply intolerable. Her pretty face took on a scowl as she restricted her eating, focusing more and more on her weight. Insisting she was fat and, therefore, bad and ugly, she began to numb out the ups and downs of adolescent life with alcohol or by sliding a razor blade across her forearm. She had to be perfect for the boys, yet she avoided them, creating more loneliness and depression.

If Cynthia had learned about the power of healthy grief and toxic shame, things might have been quite different. Without the ability to listen to the messages of her grief and the false beliefs driving her shame, without the energy of her feelings to make life worth living, she had to resort to an addictive existence to get her through the anxiety of her days and the depression of her long nights.

On a racial level, insult and injury harbored over generations explode into genocide. Anxieties and fears not faced, or understood, isolate us or push us over the edge of paranoid violence. As long as we are not emotionally clear, we really have not limped very far beyond primitive times of freeze, flee or fight. When ignorance and prejudice rather than emotional responsibility prevail, atrocities occur.

Listening to the radio on the way home from work several days ago, I heard the story of two men in the vicinity of Washington, D.C. who got into a verbal sparring match from their cars in the middle of rush hour traffic. They eventually pulled off the highway to settle things. One man was stabbed, the other shot in the stomach. The inability to manage their emotions and the lack of awareness of the frustration, shame and fear that probably seethed underneath their reactivity led to one more case of road rage.

Multiply this incident across a culture and between races and you have the shocking reality of "racial cleansing". Whether it is in the form of a Hitler, a Ku Klux Klan, African genocide or a neighborhood segregated from different ethnicities or from homes for those with developmental disabilities, the cause and result is the same. Fear, shame, and unresolved grief, often built up and inherited across generations, are fronted by anger. Anger accumulated over time becomes rage, and rage kills.

Beyond the survival that emotions help us achieve at home and at work, there is also a thriving, an expanded life made possible through the wisdom and energy of our feelings. When we fail to recognize and tolerate the fear and anxiety of stepping out, of becoming the best version of ourselves, we ignore and smother the calling each of us has to make our lives and our world a little bit better. We do not recognize, understand, or question the fears and often don't even hear the voice of attraction, of passion that speaks to us through feelings. We cheat ourselves, believing we can do it all sufficiently on one leg.

In *Return to Love*, author and teacher Marianne Williamson writes, "Our deepest fear is not that we are inadequate. Our deepest fear is that we are powerful beyond measure. It is our light, not our darkness, that most frightens us....Your playing small doesn't serve the world...As we are liberated from our own fear, our presence automatically liberates others."

Basketball was one of my greatest passions, particularly in high school. Being small and quick, I was the ball mover, now known as the point guard, when we hosted a rival seminary team in our old Brooklyn gym. The game was close, I stood on the perimeter of the other team's zone defense and looked for options. Not finding any, I took a long shot and it gracefully sailed through the air into an opponent's possession. Our six-foot-plus coach, Fr. O'Connell, jumped off the bench and screamed within several feet from my face, "I ought to punch you in the nose!"

I rarely took outside shots after that. If I did, it was with a fear that predestined the shot to miss anyway. It was over thirty years after that game before I finally took the risk of shooting the long ones. When I took up the game again in my early fifties, I began to recognize the power of the fear of embarrassment as well as anger that insisted on taking back what I had given away. Guided by a hard-won conviction that "You're never too old for new moves," I worked hard on a three-point jump shot. In another close game, this time at a local YMCA, my team was within one basket of winning. Once again, I had the ball. No options, opponent guarding me close up. Man to man. Three-point range. I faked him into taking one step back, pulled up, and let fly what felt like the longest shot I'd ever taken.

It was a strange sensation, something like breaking a sacred rule and waiting for disaster to strike. As the ball traveled towards the basket, it felt as if I were in a trance, disconnected from the leather orb leaving my hands. It ripped through the basket, all net, and we went home winners. Even if I hadn't scored, my willingness to face and work with my emotions would have made me a winner for reaching beyond a place where an unchallenged fear of being shamed had held me hostage for decades.

Whether in sports, at home, or at work, we often fear being too much, taking up too much space. A client enters our session furious at her coworkers for usurping much of the time and energy at a department meeting.

"Did you say anything or object at all?"

"Well, no. I couldn't do *that*!"

Underneath the anger is that fear of stepping out, risking our voice, our uniqueness. We don't notice, nor do we take responsibility for, the fear of showing our unmasked self. This is akin to the sun being too nervous to shine.

UNDERBELLY

Imagine:
Sunrise,
broad chest of rippling light,
tiptoeing
up the stairs,
creeping
over horizon's darkened edge,
fearing
to be seen?

We don't want the pain of feelings and, at times, we even avoid the exhilaration of positive emotion. Our bodies suffer, our relationships crash, our heads spin with anxiety, our hearts drown in depression, and our jobs choke the life out of us: one huge price to pay for the short-term gain of denying feelings. We don't want to see what's there, but while our heads are buried in the sand, life in its many forms is very apt to come along and boot us in the behind.

The results of this emotional negligence and illiteracy are profound. Over sixty percent of ailments that patients present in their doctor's office are stress related, and a great part of stress has to do with unattended, stockpiled emotional energy in the body. Migraines, ulcers, grinding teeth, high blood pressure, numerous digestive problems, neck and back tension, and heart irregularities can often be traced to a lack of emotional awareness and emotional honesty, because body, mind and emotion all work as one integrated system.

As we survey the fallout of emotional negligence, we discover three critical reasons for having feelings at all. The first is that feelings serve as our radar in the world. We must be able to receive the signals that tell us that we may have been violated (anger), that we may have violated someone else (guilt), or that we have lost someone or something (sadness, grief). We need to be aware that there may be someone or something that might harm us (fear), and it is crucial to be able to rejoice (joy, happiness) and to look forward to things (enthusiasm, excitement). These signals not only inform us, but motivate us as well, which brings us to a second reason for having feelings.

Emotions get us going. They are motivators, embodied energy, as we will later see. Anger, for example, gives us the impetus to protect and speak up for ourselves when necessary; guilt motivates us to make amends. Without the energy of these two emotions, we become targets in one case and sociopaths in the other.

Finally, emotions serve as powerful connectors between people. In marriages and close relationships, emotional honesty creates bonding, trust and openness. Even when the emotion shared is anger or disappointment, if it is an honest expression and not communicated with the intent to do damage, then we begin to bridge the gap created by our sense of violation. "The mind creates the abyss; the heart has to cross it."

A mechanic at a local car dealership was giving some marital advice to one of the salespeople who happened to be a client of mine and who was having problems at home. The mechanic also wondered why his own wife didn't feel connected to him.

"You know, I think women just want us to be too emotional all the time," he said.

"How do you mean?" the salesman asked.

"Well, she wants me to tell her that I love her. Says I don't say it enough. But I told her when we got married eighteen years ago that I loved her and that if anything ever changed, she'd be the first to know."

On the side of his lunch pail, a bumper sticker read: "I'm not insensitive; I just don't care." And because of this not caring, the gap in his marriage grew wider on a daily basis.

WHY DO WE HAVE FEELINGS?

Reason 1: Feelings are our radar, our navigating system in the world. They let us know whether things are okay or not.

Reason 2: Feelings are motivators, energizers.

Reason 3: Feelings are necessary for authentic and intimate connection with others.

Are you getting the picture? Not only are we unable to use this system to navigate the sensitive waters of relationships and to work competently as well as in balance, but we rob ourselves of the very motivators that give us the liftoff into new possibilities. At this point in the unfolding of the human species, there are personal, interpersonal and global stakes dependent upon what psychologist Daniel Goleman has called emotional intelligence. We can no longer afford to be so emotionally inept. To do so has become too painful and too dangerous.

One of the greatest legacies we can leave our children and our world is the capacity to notice, tolerate, manage, understand and express feelings--the capacity to create a truly lived life, a legacy of emotional competence and emotional integrity. And the first step in the direction of this legacy, the first step in the journey of a thousand feelings, is to dig down and find the courage to feel.

Chapter 2:

What They Are and How They Work

If feelings are to play such a central role in our lives, it makes sense that we not only understand why we have them, but what they are and how they operate. The emphasis in this chapter will be on a functional description of the nature and process of emotions. In other words, how do they work? Without such an understanding, emotions are misunderstood as intruders and barred from the events and interchanges of our daily lives. And if we're not using our radar, there's a good chance we're going to crash.

People do this in a number of ways. For years, Justine didn't attend to her feelings of boredom and frustration with her husband, until the marriage was so empty that nothing was able to fill the gap between them. Sydney neglected his anger and sense of self-betrayal every day as he dragged himself into his job. He began to show up for work late, moved around the workplace with a cloud over his head. He was eventually fired for performing poorly at the job he simply hated. Cynthia lit up whenever she played her piano and sang her songs. She disregarded the excitement that her music elicited, following in the footsteps of her parents into an accounting career that led to an ongoing depression. When she was dealing with the loss of both of her parents, Lynn needed support from her closest friends, but was not good at asking. She covered her grief with anger at her friends for not stepping forward and knowing what she needed. She withdrew, leaving her friends wondering why they never heard from her.

I once heard emotions described as land mines, ready to go off when triggered. I find that description too narrow and too militaristic. I would suggest the notion of radar or a GPS (global positioning system). Feelings are essentially reactors, as shown in the chart below. They don't react, however, in some pure and uninfluenced manner, but through a lens, through the way we perceive and think about whatever is being experienced.

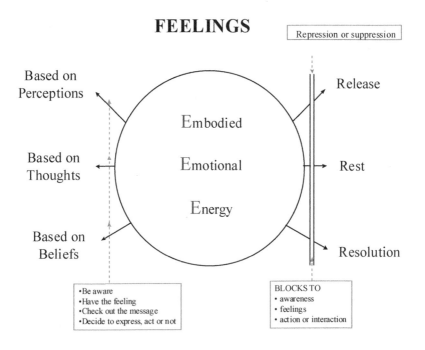

FEELINGS

Repression or suppression

Based on Perceptions

Based on Thoughts

Based on Beliefs

Embodied

Emotional

Energy

Release

Rest

Resolution

•Be aware
•Have the feeling
•Check out the message
•Decide to express, act or not

BLOCKS TO
• awareness
• feelings
• action or interaction

I'm standing on a street corner. Someone accidentally bumps into me. My radar system kicks in, registering some surprise, alerting me to pay attention. As soon as I'm able to check out the situation and find it to be harmless, the alarm subsides, returns to a state of equilibrium, and both of us can go our merry way.

However, if I'm having a bad day and someone accidentally bumps into me, I think: "That S.O.B. did it on purpose...! [grumble, grumble]" Then a different signal kicks in. Instead of surprise, the radar system sets off the anger alert due to a sense of possible violation. If I continue to think and assume negatively, the anger will remain. If I do a reality check and recognize that it was just an accident, my new perception will hopefully override the unfounded assumptions and the anger will subside.

Then again, if I've been conditioned to believe that I must always please others, must always get approval, must always take care of others first, then I get a different signal and different outcome. As soon as the accidental bumping occurs, and given the presence of a self-sacrificing belief, my radar system can only react with a guilty signal. I now respond, "Oh, oh, my fault! My fault! Sorry, sorry..." Once again, a reality check of the situation might lead to a perception that would override the guilt and let it simply be experienced as an accident. Or not.

The point is that the situation is exactly the same. However, depending upon the perception, thought or belief that is operating--the "lens" through which we view the experience--our emotional system will react differently. This is the point where many would say, "You see! You just can't trust your feelings! They're so illogical; you can't rely on the buggers!"

Feelings, I would claim to the contrary, are always doing their job. It is the way we perceive, think/assume, or believe that is often the root of the problem. Feelings are the emotional radar that signals us to check things out and, possibly, to take action or find expression.

Anxiety can be a good example of this. In her mid-forties, Sally still parents a son who is twenty years old. He probably stopped maturing emotionally when he was about twelve, when a bipolar illness activated and brought him to the point of serious drug use, violence towards his parents and himself and, most alarmingly, to the edge of suicide by the time he was fifteen. Whenever her son fails to contact her or be where he is supposed to be, Sally's anxiety level shoots through the roof, not knowing if she is going to find him dead or get the phone call that begins with, "Are you the mother of.....?" Her signal anxiety serves a very important purpose here, and Sally must respond to her radar to see if her son is still alive.

At other times, anxiety is a false alarm that nevertheless needs to be checked out. Madeleine, in her early forties, had experienced an auto accident years earlier in which a green sixteen-wheeler smashed into the back of her car as she was waiting for a red light to change. She and her five-year-old daughter were violently tossed around the inside of their vehicle as it flipped through the air and came to a crashing stop against a brick wall. Six years later, her anxiety sounds an extreme alarm, taking away her breath and causing her to become nauseous, any time a truck comes up behind her as she is driving. If the other vehicle is green, she has to pull over, often throwing up at the side of the road before she can continue.

Like sentinels warning us and catalyzing us into action, feelings are necessary and often powerful, yet require us to check the validity of our perceptions and interpretations. Otherwise we have a hijacking, as Daniel Goleman calls it, of the entire knowing-and-response system by the emotions. We will take a closer look at this shortly.

In addition to being reactions, feelings can be further understood as the triple **E's**. Feelings are **energy**, experienced in the body (**embodied**), that need to move through and away (**e-motion**) from the initial point of activation: **embodied, emotional energy**. The importance of these aspects will become more evident in subsequent chapters. For now, remember that without the energetic aspect of feelings, we remain inactive and immobile.

Given this physical, energetic nature of emotions, we need to provide channels through which they can move to a place of rest, resolution or release. We might call this *having* your feelings, or being able to *tolerate and manage* them. Despite the popular belief that we can just forget about feelings, ignored, denied or buried emotions become embodied energetic stockpiles. They're buried, but buried alive. The more they are held back and accumulate, the more they are ready to explode, implode or cause physical dis-ease. Disowned sadness can readily grow into depression and/or physical collapse; anger withheld repeatedly often becomes rage, depression and/or musculoskeletal conditions. Anger denied, however, can also result in immobility and inaction.

Jackie learned never to feel, much less show, anger. Her father seemed to express enough anger for the entire family. She watched his temper intimidate her mother on a daily basis. Her mother eventually took to misusing her anxiety medication and alcohol and was then railed at by her husband for being a worthless addict. Jackie learned this lesson well, and went on to marry abusive males. Regardless of the amount of advice she would get from friends and therapists, she never spoke up. She had no access to the anger that would motivate her to leave her relationships or at least to tell her partner to take a long walk on a short pier.

The resolution of the emotional energy can occur in many ways, which we will explore in more detail in subsequent chapters. For now, that resolution can occur through the simple, yet profound, act of awareness, or via words, tears, writing or taking action. When this occurs, the natural cycle of (1) perception of event, (2) radar response, (3) attention, (4) reality check, and (5) energetic resolution comes to an end, preparing the way for a clean experiential slate. When we honor this organic cycle, we avoid the buildup and negative life-bias that prevents us from truly being in the present. Our emotional system resets itself and proceeds to guide us through the waters of life-as-it-is.

WHAT ARE FEELINGS?

I. **Feelings are radar reactions through the lens of perception, thought or belief that let us know that things are okay or not.**

> **II. They are embodied, emotional (on the move) energy motivating us and**
>
> **III. In need of rest, resolution or release.**

Over the past decade there has been fascinating research that shows us how emotions work physiologically. It's a brain thing. In *Emotional Intelligence*, Daniel Goleman gives an excellent description of how feelings are set in motion by the brain. I have condensed his explanation below.

The brain has evolved in three stages, creating a triune or three-part brain. The oldest part of the brain, at times called the reptilian brain because of its resemblance to the primitive brain found in snakes, regulates functions such as breathing and heart rate. In addition to the reptilian part of the brain, there is the limbic brain, associated mostly with emotional experience. Finally, we have the pre-frontal cortex, the most recently evolved area of the brain, often referred to as the "grey matter," associated with thinking, analyzing, and orienting events in space and time.

Information enters our brain through the senses. This information is then channeled to a switchboard called the thalamus, which sends it to various parts of the brain for interpretation and decision making. For us to finally take action, however, we need motivating. And this is where the emotions enter. Without them, no one decision would have import for us over another. We would sit around, having come to many brilliant decisions, yet doing nothing. Not unlike Jackie in the example above.

The limbic system is home of a part of the brain known as the amygdala. The amygdala is the frontline emotional sentinel for our entire system. It gets the incoming information faster than other brain areas because its job is to immediately screen the newly received data and determine whether there is a survival need to freeze, flee or fight. It can react and then send out stress signals to the rest of our system that mobilizes our breathing, heart rate, skeletal and muscular apparatus to do what needs to be done. Without this part of the brain, we would not have survived as a species. It reacts when there is no time to think. But herein lies its Achilles heel.

In an ideal world, the amygdala would receive its information and wait patiently for the rest of the brain, particularly the pre-frontal cortex, to go over the data, review possible action and collaborate in coming to a decision. Just like a corporate board of directors. The problem arises, however, when the data is actually pointing to, *or reminding us of, past* danger. When this occurs, the amygdala hijacks the corporate board, makes a snap survival judgment, and gets the entire corporation enlisted in actions that are not always needed. Recall Madeleine and her reaction to the sight of a green truck in her rearview mirror.

There are times when we need to respond immediately. The thought of drowning, for example, has always frightened me. Yet, although my wife and most of my children can swim better than I, I would not hesitate for a moment to jump into the water if they needed help (despite being called "Bay Dork" and seeing them swim in the opposite direction when I "threaten" to enter the water and save them). In such a situation, it is the amygdala taking over when there is no time to think.

In most cases, however, even when the alarm system kicks in, it is better to refrain from reacting until the rest of the brain has had time to play its own part and give feedback. Madeleine needs to allow her logical brain to orient her to "when and where" she is at the moment. She needs to recognize the hijacking taking place. This is what I have referred to as "checking out" the perceptions, thoughts or beliefs.

I would also emphasize, however, the need to first attend to and be aware of the feeling, because it might be telling us something and trying to motivate us to positive action. If Jackie had been able to access her anger, she might have saved her body some black and blue marks and her heart some breaking.

As you can see from the brain research, emotions are very physical events, not only in their brain origin, but also in how we experience them and how they motivate us. They have been with us for thousands of years and have been a major reason for our survival as a species. It is now our task to become **conscious experts** about our own system of feelings. This means balancing mind and heart, involving the "thinking" part of the brain to complement the "feeling" part, to avoid what many refer to as "overreacting" or uncontrolled emotion. It also demands a respect for and an honoring of the energetic, guidance system that not only teaches and motivates us to take care of ourselves, but also reveals to us what we want, what makes us happy, and what makes us come alive.

EMOTIONAL TASKS

I. Honor and attend to the feelings

II. Balance mind and heart

PART TWO

The Four Steps to Emotional Honesty

Introduction

Consider yourself in training. Emotional competence is not something you can simply read about. You have to do it.

I have developed and tested, over many years of personal and clinical experience, a four-step method that evolved from a course in stress management I once taught. I had been invited by a Fortune 500 company to create this course and was delivering one of the classes on emotions to a group of researchers and scientists, folks not known for spontaneous bursts of emotional truth. One of the participants asked, "Can you give us *steps* as to how to do this?"

I had just spent the entire class focusing on the process of *being* with feelings in any given moment, and he wanted *steps*! For a moment, I wanted to choke him. But knowing the importance of checking out my impulse and preventing an emotional hijacking, I thought over his request and promised to get back to him.

Despite the fact that he was asking for a "procedure" for when and what to do, something that felt too rigid for a living, breathing process, I realized that there could be a creative balance between structure and process. Emotions were foreign territory for this researcher, and he needed a map and signposts to help him navigate his way through. Despite his Ph.D., he had to be educated.

What I brought back to that class the following week and what I have taught my clients ever since makes up the major portion of Part II of this book. The four steps must be practiced and used (exercises accompany each chapter). Rather than being asked to learn a curriculum for its own sake, you are, as mentioned above, in training. You are about to embark upon a path, a *way* of living with your heart as well as your mind. This takes nothing less than a daily commitment to these four steps, which, although not the territory, will transform stumbling into directed growth. These steps will lead you out of the cellar of knee-jerk living into the daylight of intentional behavior and deepened connection to yourself, your work and your loved ones.

This is a promise.

Chapter 3:

Step One – Awareness of the Feeling

But, tragically, most people never get to see
that all is well because they are asleep.
They are having a nightmare.

Anthony de Mello

The Fable of Simon the Turle

The sun rises, peeks slowly over the hill and begins to warm the tall grasses, still wet with the moisture that has settled in during the night. Light slips through the brush and falls upon something hard, something motionless.

Simon can feel the warmth of daybreak begin to penetrate his home. He doesn't move for quite a while, making sure that things around him are in order. Box turtles are like that.

He was incubated and hatched from an egg and quickly moved into a shell. Something inside told him that things in general weren't safe. Nothing was certain except that one could easily become someone's turtle soup if not careful. Simon's mother, an anxious sort, modeled this viewpoint to perfection. Protective, watchful, knowing that there were all sorts of things out there that could roll a turtle over in an instant, she taught Simon the way of caution, preferring to be safe than sorry.

"Time for something to eat," he thinks, and begins his slow, deliberate routine of looking a foot or two around him, searching for insects and juicy blades of grass. His world is not very large. As soon as he finds his breakfast, he goes back to his spot, pulls his head back inside and notices nothing more than the old contented feeling after a meal or that familiar nervous feeling that tells him never to let down his shell. You just never know... Simon knows very little of what is around him, and even less of the occasional reactions that whisper that he's trapped and that parents aren't always right.

"No, no!" he always insists to himself. "My shell is safe. It's a good box. Mom knows what she's talking about!" To be continued...

*****

I often tell a story about a prince who was born and raised in one room of a castle. He was kept there to make sure that he was raised properly, as well as safely, with no outside influences to contaminate him. There were no windows in the room, only a door beyond which he had never taken a step.

For the prince, life around him was this room. Life consisted of the few reactions to the daily basics of eating, sleeping and receiving praise from his royal parents.

Our prince was unaware that there were other magnificent rooms in the castle: ballrooms, dining halls, and courtyards. There were dragons to slay, damsels to impress. He had no sense of a world beyond the castle's moat. From time to time, however, something inside stirred him. He hadn't the words for it, but it *felt* like being left behind, it *felt* incomplete. That's when something in his gut would heat up--dissatisfaction with what his parents had created for him. Then something else in his stomach sank when he thought at all negatively about his loving parents. He couldn't move. He was frozen in fear. But he had no words for any of this, because he had no awareness. Without awareness, he had no clue, and, being clueless, stayed stuck in his limited world.

Without awareness, we live our lives in a box, in a sheltered room, not even knowing that there is any other way. With our busyness, preoccupations and conditioning, we are often out of touch with what surrounds us: moments, things, people. We have even less sense of what is taking place inside, particularly our emotional radar. Without attention to what is inside and outside, we exist in ways that are, at best, very limiting and, at worst, painfully repetitive and damaging.

Buddhist tradition refers to this attention as *mindfulness*: mindful of each moment, each action, each sensation both internally and externally generated. Noticing, paying attention, and observing are all synonymous of mindfulness. We exist quite often in the very limited darkness of automatic living. Awareness is the light out of that pattern of living.

And it is, as mentioned before, a way of being in the world. It is not something to be turned on and off occasionally, but requires daily practice, as well as courage. It is the first of the four steps and possibly the single most important living skill you will gain from this book. But only if you practice. Remember, you are in training, training to take back and unfold your life, much as Simon and our prince must do. There is so much more to life than we think, stuck as we often are in our boxes of limited awareness. Emotions will lead us to the larger picture, and awareness is the first step to be taken.

We begin with the practice of awareness of what is around us, what our senses are telling us.

AWARENESS OF WHAT IS "OUTSIDE"

- Begin by noticing everything around you that comes into your awareness **visually**. See if anything "grabs your attention," e.g., an object, shape, color.

- Do the same with **auditory sensations.**

- **And with tactile experience** (clothing against your skin, air movement, chair against your legs and back, hand sensations).

- Notice if there is any **scent or smell** that enters awareness.

- Take sixty seconds to be aware of all sensory input—just where you are!

- Repeat as often as you can throughout the day, wherever, whenever.

It takes courage to be aware. It requires that we make the commitment to step outside our autopilot way of living. Autopilot living is like falling into a turbulent river, caught up in the white rapids, crashing into rocks, and being tossed around with all kinds of debris. As the river carries you downstream, you notice the branch of a large tree that extends from the river's edge several feet across the rushing waters. As you pass under the branch, you grab onto it, pull yourself out, and sit down on the bank. Catching your breath, you look at the river, noticing, observing, glad that you are no longer caught up in the stuff that whirls by. This is what awareness does for us. It gets us out of the rapids and onto a solid bank. It lets us observe, rather than be swept into the torrents of daily busyness.

A great deal of that "debris" is input from the outside. Sometimes the input is toxic, sometimes it's just too much, and it begins to overwhelm us. And if we're not paying attention, we get caught in the torrent.

Recently, I was sitting in a chiropractor's office, waiting for my treatment. I became aware of grey colors, magazines flaunting commercials of perfect (and starved) bodies, and music pumped in from a local radio station that produced as much mindless banter as it did jarring music. I began to notice my irritability and an urge to get up and leave.

This input was too much and toxic at the same time. As soon as I was aware of the impact of it all on my internal system, I shifted my focus to a magazine article that took me to a town in Alaska. Without awareness, I would not have been able to screen out the atmosphere and shift my attention. In doing so, I could feel the internal change for the better.

On the other hand, there are times when we don't appreciate our environment enough, because we are running on automatic. Driving down the highway, we are often engrossed in mental activity, resulting in unawareness of the passing scenery. Several exits down the pike, something in us notices the exit sign that we don't want to miss. We snap back to the present and get off the highway.

We do this when we walk, more intent upon what we are mulling over or fantasizing about in our heads, more focused on where we want to go than on the going. I've often encouraged clients to take a "gratitude walk." It's interesting how noticing what enters our awareness through the senses so readily leads to appreciating the objects of our perception.

Walking down a street filled with shops, I often appreciate the colors, objects, faces, sounds, smells. At times, I'm filled with gratitude for the very act of seeing, hearing, smelling, or touching. Walking itself is no longer an automatic act, blurred like scenery from a speeding car. It steps forward in my awareness, becoming a gift for which I feel gratitude.

Interestingly, awareness is not only the first line of defense against toxicity and overload from the "outside." It also allows us to more deeply penetrate life around us with an attitude of savoring and gratefulness. Awareness is like a stage awaiting entrances from life itself, in all its ordinary and extra-ordinary forms.

AWARENESS OF WHAT IS "INSIDE"

- Notice your **breathing**, where it enters and leaves the body, and all the sensations connected with it. Be aware of the pauses, the still points, at the peak of each in-breath and the end of each out-breath.

- Then, shift the lens of your awareness to your **body**. Scan it from the top of your head to the tips of your fingers and toes, noting any sensations, pleasurable or not. Do all of this without changing anything.

- Next, attend to your **thoughts**. Do your best to watch them, rather than getting caught up in them. It sometimes helps to name them: worry thoughts, busy thoughts, planning thoughts, attack thoughts, etc.

- Notice any **feelings or emotions** that might be active. Observe where they are taking place in your body. Notice if there is any name that goes with them: sadness, anger, etc.

- Finally, be still and allow your awareness to watch **whatever** comes onto the stage of your inner perception for the next sixty seconds. It might also be **images or memories** that are asking for attention.

If you were on a boat, fishing or getting a tan, you might not notice that you were about to get stuck on a reef. The boat's radar would indicate this, but you wouldn't be paying attention. In the same way, if we do not attend to the internal signals from our breath, body sensations, thoughts, emotions, images, we simply won't get the messages they have for us. We've got the equipment, but we're not using it.

This is particularly true of awareness of our emotions. The courage to be aware of them and to notice them is of utmost importance. (Simon and the Prince didn't have much courage.) The body sensation is usually our first clue that something emotional is going on. A tightness in the throat or chest, a watery sensation behind the eyes, nausea, a knot in the stomach, pain in the neck, headache, tingling—all can be indicators that there is a feeling asking for attention, trying to tell us something.

"Notice what you notice," a former mentor of mine would say. I rarely begin sessions by asking people, "What are you feeling?", because they usually *think about,* rather than *observe* and *be with* their emotions. I typically ask, "What do you notice going on in your body?" From there, it is usually easier to put a name on the feeling and, most importantly, to be aware of it rather than think it to death.

This awareness (Step 1) can then lead to being with the feeling (Step 2), which opens us to an experience of the emotion (precisely what many of us want to avoid). These first steps then make it possible to check out the emotional message (Step 3) and, if needed, be motivated into action (Step 4). For our own good, it is important to remember that every feeling has a reason for being present, and every feeling has the right to life.

Even though our first reaction to a "bad" or "uncomfortable" feeling might be to ignore it, remember the box that both Simon and the prince were in without a clue they were in one. We do the same in our day-to-day existence when we ignore the feedback system that tells us what is going on in the inner and outer world of our lives. We think we're taking care of ourselves and being "nice" to others by banishing emotions from our awareness, but instead we are choking off the life and the possibilities we might be living. We're convinced that we are getting on with life, but we are living a fantasy, disconnected from our guidance system. At worst, we are asleep, having a nightmare.

PRACTICE

- Take a walk, being aware of input from each sense, one at a time: seeing, hearing, tactile feeling, smelling. Appreciate what enters your awareness, as well as the act of sensing itself.

- Be mindful of every sensation during the first few bites of each meal this week.

- Before you sleep, when you awake, and several times during the day, practice the "60-second break" by taking one minute to be aware of all internal stimuli (breath, body sensations, feelings, thoughts, images).

- In a small notebook, jot down your observations, being particularly aware of emotions and where you notice them in your body. It's not necessary to give them a name, if you're stumped after "mad, glad or sad." Just observe the sensations and their location.

Chapter 4:

Step Two – Being with the Feeling

**I dreamed I roared
like a lion
with a sound
that shook my chest....**

**And the voice said,
"Dream, dream
onward."**

Simon the Turtle began to poke his head a bit further out of his shell. He was noticing things now: things around him as well as things inside him. It was a sunny afternoon when he dozed off, watching birds, colors, sky and clouds...and dreamed. He dreamt he was a lion living inside his shell, trying to roar, but couldn't. It was too tight, too cramped. He awoke *suddenly and felt a pushing and a longing, but he had no words for it. He only knew it wouldn't go away.*

The birds, colors, skies and clouds he was noticing didn't go away either. They became pictures, taking up residence inside his head. He began to think about the strangest thing. Strange, at least, for a turtle. He wanted those wonderful pictures inside him to last forever. He wanted everyone else to see them the way he did. He actually began to see himself...

"No, no," he thought. "That is just too weird for a turtle. After all, I have to live in my shell."

But those images wouldn't leave him. He dreamed again, this time of leaving his shell behind, feeling quite naked, and following the beautiful things of the world and...and, drawing and painting them! He awoke remembering a turtle without a shell, on a journey with no destination, carrying an enormous pencil over his shoulder.

"Oh, oh! Weird, bad, bad, weird! Turtle-soup time! " he worried.

Yet the feelings pushing and straining inside his body wouldn't let up. He didn't have names for them, since turtles don't pay much attention to things outside, much less things inside. He couldn't tell his mother about the dreams or what was happening inside him. She would just tell him to ignore them and be content inside his shell, where things were safe and sure. Yet, the more he was aware of those pushings and yearnings, those fears and the excitement, the more he knew things would never be the same...

*****

Isn't that what we often fear the most? That things will change, perhaps change forever. Charles Dubois wrote: "The important thing is to be able, at any moment, to sacrifice what we are for what we could become." Yet even "good" feelings can scare us as much as the "bad" ones.

So feelings are often ignored or buried. Yet they are the movement of life inside us. The emotion knocking on your door is letting you know that you have reason to be excited or fearful and that your aliveness is calling you to a larger version of yourself. Both negative and positive emotions can be unnerving invitations to get real. They ask us to attend to what we want or don't want in our lives, to what is good or not good for us. They ask us to hold onto ourselves.

In the thirteenth century, the Persian poet Rumi wrote:

The Guest House

> This being human is a guest house.
> Every morning a new arrival.
>
> A joy, a depression, a meanness,
> Some momentary awareness comes
> As an unexpected visitor.
>
> Welcome and entertain them all!
> Even if they are a crowd of sorrows,
> who violently sweep your house
> empty of its furniture,
> still treat each guest honorably.
> He may be clearing you out
> for some new delight….

Always, there is a purpose for feelings, but we cannot listen (Step One), much less react if needed (Step Four), if we are not able to *be with* the feeling. This is what is meant by "tolerating" or managing the emotion, rather than being overwhelmed by or denying it. As my mentor would often say, "You must learn to be strong in all of your emotions." It is our task to stand on the firm ground of emotional awareness and emotional being. From this place we can journey forth with our guidance system, listening to our anger when we've been violated or to our guilt when we've truly wronged another, feeling the truth of sadness, or delighting in the joy of a relationship or job that fulfills us.

If Simon doesn't find the courage to feel what is happening inside him, he will go back to his shell. This courage will require the awareness of and the capacity to be with his feelings. He needs to tolerate happiness, joy, expanded living, for it is often the fear of being too much or of being disappointed again that drives us back into the shell of our comfort zone, where we know what to expect.

Betty spent her childhood in the shadow of an older brother who was born with Downs Syndrome. Her parents struggled in every way imaginable in order to create a life for her brother, leaving Betty invisible. She tried to be the perfect child who never upset her parents, who never expressed a need. They had enough to deal with.

She grew up and married a man who bullied her verbally and emotionally, relying on her inability to speak up or to ask for what she wanted. She developed anorexia and compulsive housecleaning in order to feel some kind of control whenever she felt the anger, lack of control and invisibility that had lived just below the surface, but could never be revealed.

She finally divorced her husband, and now, 43 years old, she sits across from me, wondering why she still isn't able to speak up to her mother.

"Betty, what's the worst thing that would happen if you spoke up to your mother?" I ask.

"She would get angry!"

"And then?"

"I'd get a little scared, and I'd feel *bad*!"

"What kind of bad?"

I gave her plenty of time, figuring that she would have trouble with the "g" word.

"Guilty."

Guilt, which easily slides into shame, was at the bottom of her inability to speak up. How different her life will be as she learns to tolerate the guilt signal. Tolerating it will entail paying attention to the feeling and, at times, managing it by releasing some of its intensity. This sets the stage for listening to what the feeling has to say. If, instead of tolerating and listening, she avoids or denies the emotion, then she will become imprisoned, rather than guided, by it.

Sharon, on the other hand, had a hard time tolerating her excitement and joy. Attractive, bright, and moving up the corporate ladder, she came to me because she was miserable and depressed. She had a loving husband, an engineer whose parents had accepted her as their own. They had three wonderful children. All of this was in stark contrast to her childhood, when she lived in a dreary apartment at the edge of Detroit with a mood-disordered mother. Her father abandoned them when Sharon was seven.

"I must be crazy! I've got everything a woman would want, and still I'm miserable. It's gotten to the point that I don't even want my husband to touch me. I feel so guilty!"

"Has anything changed?" I ask.

"I'm not sure. I mean, he's wonderful and all. Maybe that's part of the problem. He's so damned nice! The other thing is that I don't need him like I used to. I can support myself now, not like when we got married, when he swooped in like a knight on a white horse. Maybe it's an age thing. Do marriages go through midlife crises?"

Sharon had grown while her husband had remained in the same developmental place: nice, responsible, and predictable, particularly in bed. She had also discovered a sense of passion. She loved watching couples salsa dancing, visiting sculpture gardens and pottery studios, or looking at exotic window displays of travel agencies.

Instead of honoring these feelings, she stifled them and became depressed herself. None of her aliveness fit into the story she and her husband created when they married. Instead of marrying in order to bring out the best in herself and her husband, she had married to gain what she was missing: security, predictability, and family. She had entered a deficit-based relationship. Now she is depressed because she is ignoring the emotional signals telling her to grow.

Sharon is at a crossroads: listen to her guidance system and insist on changes in the marriage or live with the way things are, avoid all of those feelings, but choose to remain unhappy. There are times when listening to the positive emotions of excitement and joy might mean change, might mean disrupting the system, but to deny the call is to deny who we are. And that never works. We fear the unknown, we fear the fear, we fear the judgment of others, and we fear our own guilt and shame. The way out of such dilemmas, the way into true living, is not always easy, but it is absolutely possible.

"How To" with The L.I.D.S. Concept

Emotional energy is like a wave that wants to pass through us. It will do just that if we don't set up obstacles to the natural flow of the feelings. Whether we overtly deny or bury the feelings or subtly deflect them, the result will be the same: a stockpile that wants out and will create all kinds of disturbances in our body, since it is the body that must hold back the physical energy of the emotions. Blocked emotional flow can easily lead to a tsunami of feelings that overwhelms us. So we shut down even more, stockpile more, and fear our feelings even more.

Ideally, emotions flow like a river. Without banks, a river can become a destructive, frightening force of nature. Within its banks, a river is a thing of beauty and creative power. Steps One (awareness of the feeling) and Two (being with the feeling) serve as the banks of our emotional rivers.

Being with a feeling is necessary in order for us to learn from the feeling. At times, we may also need to manage emotional intensity before we can work with the feeling. I have developed a four-step process called L.I.D.S, to help you accomplish Step Two.

The first step is to **Locate** the feeling. The feeling takes place in the body, so you typically experience the emotion as a physical sensation. Where is it in your body? In your face? Jaw? Chest? Belly? Neck? Shoulders? Arms? Legs? Buttocks? Genitals? Hands? Feet?

The second step of L.I.D.S. is to determine the **Intensity** of the feeling and how intense you want it to be so you can move on with your life. Ask yourself what I often ask clients: "On a scale of 0-10, with zero representing no feeling at all and ten representing the strongest you've ever felt this feeling, how strong is it now?" Then ask yourself to what level you want the feeling reduced so you can go on with your day. Now you know where you are in terms of emotional intensity and where you want to go.

These two steps give you the experience of separating yourself from the feeling. This is not denial, but the ability to observe the feeling and allow it to move through you. To allow the feeling is to free yourself into full living. To deny the feeling is to become hostage to the buried emotional energy.

Poet Robert Bly writes of the "long bag we drag behind us." It is the sack we carry over our shoulder filled with emotional baggage. Every time we ignore an emotional event, it becomes heavier. It is like holding a one-pound bag of sugar in your hand. Not a problem immediately, but over the course of a few hours it becomes unbearably heavy. This emotional weight inevitably takes a toll on you physically.

The "D" in L.I.D.S. guides you to **Describe** the emotion as you experience it in the body. How big is it? Does it have a shape? A color? A temperature? Does it move? The benefit of this is that it keeps you aware of the *experience* of the feeling. It also reinforces your position as the observer, which enables you to both be separate from the feeling and connected to it.

Finally, the "S" instructs you to **Send** the emotion out from the body. The emotional waves are now moving through the body, rather than being stuck. To send it out, you need a vehicle and a destination.

The vehicle is your *intention* to honor the feeling, learn what you can from it, and allow it to move through you, leaving you at peace, ready to express or take action. The physical form of this intention is the use of *breath* to move the emotional energy outward.

Breathe into wherever your feeling is located and on the exhale, send it out in a stream into the universe (or to a destination you have chosen). If the feeling has a color to it, imagine a stream of that color from the body outward. The destination can be "the universe," "the limitless sky" or even a container where you can store emotion for further attention in the future. The feeling is physical energy, so the vehicle needs to be physical. Breathe in through the nose and out through the mouth, as if you were breathing out through a thin straw. A long exhalation gives a sense of control and calm.

Let your eyes close and imagine some sort of container that could hold emotional energy. What material is it made of? How large is it? Shape? Thickness of the walls? How do you open and then seal it? Walk around it to make sure it doesn't leak. Now imagine opening it, and direct a stream of that emotion into the container. Continue to do that until you reach the level (0-10) that feels manageable to you. When you've done this, close the container, walk around it once more to make sure it's secure, and let your eyes slowly open.

Caution: Do not do this exercise with your eyes closed while driving, while taking part in an intimate conversation or when participating in a board meeting. People hate it when that happens...

Being With the Feeling

- **Locate the feeling**

- **Identify the intensity of the feeling**

- **Describe the feeling**

- **Send the feeling outwards**

Sending the feeling outward is a releasing, particularly if the emotions are strong and threaten to overwhelm you. During my first extended sailing experience on the choppy, fickle waters off the coast of Maine, I learned that when sudden storms hit, you don't try to stay on-course. You just try to stay afloat. The sails come down, you face into the wind and hold on until it passes.

An emotional storm needs to be handled in a similar manner. Recognize it (awareness), let go of any intentions to problem-solve or communicate, face it, breathe and release, and hold on. It will pass, and, when it does, you will learn what the experience had to teach you.

Trying to deny the storm, or any feeling for that matter, will only rob you of a radar system and block your response-ability. Understanding why the storm arose and what it was trying to tell you comes later.

Step Two requires courage and practice. As complicated as it might seem, the process can become as natural as breathing. It is being *present* to the feeling. It is being at home with your innate guidance system.

Being present to the feeling can be enhanced by naming the emotion, when possible. (Be careful of *thinking* too much about the name of emotion, since this will take you away from the experience of it). To help with naming the feeling, here is a list of one-word emotions (except for expressions such as "pissed off," which I consider a run-on word of utmost importance). Not all of these are feelings in the strict sense, but are close enough to get you started. Remember, if you can't say it in one word, it's not a feeling.

happy	glad	joyful	loving
pleased	excited	affectionate	appreciated
elated	cheerful	satisfied	thankful
confident	thrilled	peaceful	blissful
pleasant	quiet	content	loved
serene	proud	devoted	hopeful
bored	embarrassed	grumpy	sorry
miserable	distressed	worried	depressed
trapped	troubled	disorganized	mixed up
foggy	uncomfortable	undecided	uptight

put out	distrustful	lonely	guilty
worthless	validated	inadequate	scared
inadequate	disappointed	afraid	lost
hopeless	sorrowful	upset	anxious
frightened	down	panicky	threatened
insecure	uneasy	timid	unsure
nervous	apprehensive	angry	furious
mad	resentful	hurt	rejected
abandoned	betrayed	frustrated	confused
enraged	annoyed	vengeful	unwanted
unneeded	connected	accepted	ashamed
safe	isolated	cornered	shocked
vulnerable			

Some of these words refer to more "primary" feelings such as disgust, shame, and fear. Other words, such as rejected or abandoned, are really more what we perceive as happening to us, but are so charged with emotion and are so descriptive for many people, that I have included them in this list. If the feeling word you are using is more about what has happened to you, it might help to follow it up with something like, "When it seems like I've been *rejected, etc.*, I feel_____."

This leads us into the next of our four major steps: reading the message of the emotion.

PRACTICE – Being Strong in All Emotions

1. Continue on a daily basis to **practice inner and outer awareness.**

2. **Use the L.I.D.S. strategy on positive and less intense emotions** whenever they arise during the day. Try to "catch" (awareness) at least one a day and then hang out with it.

3. **Jot down in a journal or notebook what you experienced.** Include the name of the feeling if you can, where you felt it in your body, what it was in response to, and the intensity at the beginning and the end.

4. **Read over what you have written every few days or at the end of the week.** This is an important step. Here you deepen what you've learned experientially by reviewing your successes.

Chapter 5:

Step Three – Reading the Message of the Feeling

Simon was becoming a dysfunctional turtle. Usually calm, complacent, and compliant, he found himself getting irritable, edgy. His shell began to feel more like a prison than a shelter, and his mom more like a prison guard. The corner of the marshland that had been his backyard no longer interested him. His dreams haunted him, and his *feelings simply stockpiled, threatening to explode through his shell.*

He dreamed the dream of something bigger, something that felt, yes, felt as if a warm, brilliant sun were rising in his belly, then into his heart and head. He continued to see things as if for the first time, and he so wanted to share his first sight with others. He saw himself in open spaces, learning from what others in the marshland had seen and experienced, experiencing new things himself, and always drawing wonderful pictures and paintings of all that lived in the marsh, hanging them from the low branches of willow trees so others could gaze upon what they had often noticed, but perhaps, now, could really see for the first time. "Isn't that what neighbors are for?" asked the Dream Voice.

So vivid and pressing were his dreams that, upon awakening, he was never quite sure if he was ending a dream and entering the real world, or if he was leaving the real world and entering a very annoying dream. He couldn't stay, he was afraid to go. But, where? How?

Boredom, fear, frustration, and anxiety alternately began to pound and throb inside. "How did they get in there?" he wondered. "Inside my shell!?!" He wasn't happy with the outside, and even less happy on the inside.

"Why can't I just be like other turtles and be okay with what Mom told me?" he would ask himself, often aloud. One day someone overheard him, someone who would soon provide the keys and the answers to his questions and his dreams.

"Because you're not and you can't!" came a tiny voice from outside Simon's shell. Simon suddenly felt that

pull in his stomach that said, "Beware! This could be soup time!" For once, however, he didn't pull further back into his shell just because something in his belly was crying, "Danger!"

He thought, "After all, it is a small voice, so it couldn't be any bigger than me...and I could always pull back into my shell. Right?"

"Right," agreed Tiny Voice.

"Oh-h-h-h, how did it know what I was thinking? Not good, not good."

"You're doing okay," said the voice. "You paid attention to your stomach, but then you used your turtle brain to see that your stomach was upset for no good reason. Head and heart. Nice job."

The voice was sounding less and less frightening. Simon slowly moved his nose, eyes and then the rest of his head towards the opening of his shell. Peering outside, past the edge of his shell, he came nose to nose with...a t-shirt that said "Mighty Mouse."

Ronald was, to be truthful, a bit taken with himself, but, mice who can read thoughts and who know things about brains and feelings are rare. Standing on his hind legs, front feet crossed in front of his chest, Ronald's entire body was no bigger than the opening of Simon's shell.

Simon was relieved, then amused, then more than a little curious. For the first time, here in his small corner of the marshland, was the tiniest of creatures who, for some unknown reason, stirred the first bit of hope in a heart that had been heavy for a long, long time....

*****

For the first time in what is Simon's attempt to leave home, emotionally as well as physically, he is not letting himself be ruled by his feelings, but is starting to use them as the guidance system that they are meant to be. He is starting to check out the reality of whatever is triggering his emotions. And that is exactly what our third step in emotional mastery is all about.

The theme of leaving home recurs over and over throughout our lives. We do this when we leave the womb and enter the world, when we experience our first day of school, as adolescents joining our pack of peers, entering college and marriage, changing jobs, standing up for ourselves. Every time we shed an old skin and step beyond our comfort zones, we are leaving the restrictive home of our former self and stepping into an expanded experience. It is anxiety producing and exhilarating at the same time. Because of the unpredictability and uncertainty of these moments, we need tools, and primary among them is our emotional compass.

This compass is with us from birth, albeit in an undeveloped form. As infants, we cry and gurgle, indicating pain, discomfort, needs on the one hand, and pleasure, comfort, satisfaction on the other. As we grow older, this emotional energy begins to differentiate into a more sophisticated variety of signals in order to prepare us for the complexity of life experiences. Simon has begun to notice boredom, fear, frustration and anxiety, all necessary for him to assess where he is in his life's map and whether to move forward or not. In attending to and questioning these signals, he begins the marriage of clear mind and open heart.

As the poet Rumi reminds us, it is good to greet each feeling as if it were a guest at our front door. It is also important, however, to check out the visitor who might want to chat (neutral), rob us (warning) or tell us how gorgeous we are (well-being). Remember that a feeling is a *response* to internal events (thoughts, images, memories) as well as external events, but each response occurs through the *lens* of how we perceive, think or believe. Our task, consequently, is twofold: to recall the specific message of the feeling and then to do a reality check of that message, because the lens might be distorting the object of our perception.

Feeling guilty is classically one of those times when listening to the message and checking it out is crucial. Having been raised in an Irish Catholic matriarchy, I learned about guilt early on, teasing that I resented Jewish and Italian friends who claimed they had the corner on guilt-inducing. With both hands tied behind our back with a rosary, we Catholics could hold our own with the best of them.

I will relate two childhood events, and keep in mind that the message specific to guilt is that I *may have violated* someone or some code of ethics or morals.

I was seated in the third row of my fifth-grade class, right next to Billy Addison. Hunched down behind the two classmates in front of us, we were clowning around, laughing that irrepressible laugh that's reserved for places and times when it is most forbidden. Suddenly, the edgy voice of Sister Mary Valentine cut right through my protective wall of classmates and demanded, "And what's so very funny, *Mr.* Seubert? Stand up, please!"

Completely caught off guard, I stood up, awash in embarrassment, and stammered, "Sister, Billy Addison is making me laugh."

"Stop blaming other people for what you're doing, Andrew. Now be quiet and get back to work!"

"Yes, Sister," I said. I felt something besides embarrassment well up inside of me, and tried to ignore it.

After lunch, we all hung around the playground outside the school. Another classmate, Mary Jane, came up to me and said, "Billy's mad at you for blaming him in class this morning."

"So??" I defended. I was now clear about the guilt that had arisen, which was telling me that I had violated my friend and our friendship just to save my Catholic behind. Unfortunately, I hadn't grown enough into my integrity to apologize, which is what the guilt was pushing for. The message was clear and was accurate.

Flash forward a year or so. I overheard some older kids on the asphalt basketball court calling each other "scumbag." Irish Catholic mothers typically avoid colorful expletives and, in the absence of a father for most of my childhood, I was left to wondering what was so bad about this new word off the streets.

I made the mistake of approaching a parish priest, my spiritual director at the time (I was heading to the seminary years later), and blurted out, "Hey, Father, what's a 'scumbag'?"

"Well," he replied, "that's not something you need to know about right now." That same warm flush came into my face again. Guilt was on the move, but I simply assumed that I had done something wrong. I didn't know that *feeling* guilty is not the same as *being* guilty. It's a signal that needs checking out: had I really violated this priest or some code of morals by asking?

If I had known to ask that question and to check out the warning signal of guilt, the answer would have been obvious. But no one had educated me emotionally. I just assumed that *feeling* guilty equaled being guilty, and never asked a question like that again.

STEP THREE

1. **Recall the message of the feeling**
2. **Reality check the message**

Feelings, in general, are emotional responses or reactions to the way we perceive, think or believe about an internal or external event. Because many of us are fairly illiterate, emotionally speaking--comfortable mostly with "mad, glad and sad"--it's important to expand our vocabulary with an understanding of some of the messages of specific emotions.

SOME OF THE MESSAGES

ANGER – is the <u>response to a perception, thought or belief</u> that I *may* have been violated.

GUILT – is the response that I *may* have violated someone or some code of ethics or morals.

FEAR – is the response that someone or something *might* be about to harm me.

SADNESS – is the response that I *may* have lost someone or something.

SHAME – is the response that I *may* have been untrue to my core values and lessened my self.

HAPPINESS/JOY – is the response that things *may be* well with myself, the world and others.

EXCITEMENT – is the response that something good *might* be coming my way.

BOREDOM – is the response that I *may* not be getting the stimulation I require.

JEALOUSY – is the response that I *may* not be getting the acknowledgment and connection I expect from a significant other.

A special thanks to Jack Walters for introducing me to these definitions.

Once the message of the feeling is understood, our task is to check out the reliability of the response by asking creative questions, such as the following:

Anger – have I really been violated?

Guilt – have I really violated someone or some code of ethics/morals?

Sadness – what have I really lost?

Fear – is something really about to harm me? What's the worst that could happen?

Shame – have I betrayed my own core values, my Real Self? Am I really less, really damaged, really inadequate?

Essentially, we bring a clear, questioning mind to *collaborate* with the emotional system. Without the clarity of an observing mind, emotions can lead us off course, due to false perceptions, thoughts and/or beliefs. Without the energy and motivation of feelings, the mind gets stuck, defends, and plays avoidant games.

It is this collaboration that enables us to differentiate between *constructive* and *toxic* forms of a feeling. The feeling, as mentioned earlier, is always doing its job. It is the erroneous perceptions, thoughts or beliefs that can set off an emotional response that misdirects us and prevents us from dealing effectively with our environment.

Guilt and shame, by way of example, are frequent bedfellows and deserve differentiation and clarification. Guilt tells us that what we've *done* may be wrong. Shame tells us that how we *are being* may be wrong. It's the difference between a bad deed and a bad person. One says we are violating through our actions; the other says we offend our Self and others by stepping beyond the boundaries of respect for our true nature or the true nature and rights of another. These are the constructive forms of guilt and shame.

On the other hand, guilt that is driven by toxic thoughts, beliefs or perceptions becomes a false alarm. Note that it is not the guilt that is toxic. Just think of a house smoke alarm that goes off when smoke escapes from the oven. The alarm is doing its job. It just so happens that there is no fire behind the smoke. We must check out both the guilt and the smoke to make sure nothing is truly burning.

False thinking, believing or perceiving can also trigger shame. In such cases, the false message can go beyond the signal that I've been untrue to my core being, to the false belief that who I fundamentally am is damaged, flawed, inadequate. It is quite common for a guilt response to slip into a shame state, particularly when we are actually guilty. Because I *did* wrong, *therefore* who I *am* is wrong.

Gillian, the mother of three children, lost her husband after eight years of marriage when a tractor engine exploded in his face as he tried to refuel. As they drove home from the hospital, one of the children asked, "Are we going to be able to stay together, mom? Are we going to lose our home?"

Gillian committed herself to making sure that never happened. Unfortunately, she did this by using the life insurance settlement to give her children anything they wanted. As they grew older, they expected her to bail them out of life itself: out of debt, bad relationships, bad career choices, and alcoholism.

When he was in his early thirties, her oldest son would come to her, asking for money she didn't have. When she considered meeting his request, she'd have a massive guilt attack, and instead of challenging the truth of the emotional message, she would immediately give in to *avoid feeling guilty.* The "I've got to save my child at all costs" belief immediately converted into the shame-based belief, "I'm a bad mother."

Her emotional task was, and is, to have the courage to be aware of her emotions (step one), to let the feelings happen (step two) and then to check out the truthfulness of the messages (step three). In a nutshell, she has to stop being the safety net for her children because it not only keeps them from growing up, but also prevents her from having a life of her own. In side-stepping the guilt experience, she truly violates her children by not demanding the best of them, and she violates herself by remaining hostage to a fear-based belief system.

In summary, it is of utmost importance to remember that the feeling is always, yes, *always* doing its job. It is our perceptions, thoughts and beliefs that must be examined and questioned. The feeling rings our front doorbell; it is up to us to answer by opening the door and seeing what's really there.

Training Exercise

1. Take a few days off from reading this book and begin to *jot down* any of the listed feelings above that you might experience.

2. *Recall the message* that is attached to the feeling, particularly after you've let yourself *have* the feeling.

3. *Decide* whether the message is accurate or not by asking creative, clear-minded questions.

4. If the message is inaccurate, determine the source of the inaccuracy:

Perception? Thought? Belief?

5. In any case, *thank* **the messenger emotion for doing its job, and thank your brain for collaborating.**

Chapter 6:

Step Four: Deciding to Act, Express...
Or Not

Simon's head was out, no longer stuck up his shell. He had been out before, but just for a short while, and just to make his way around the small corner of the swamp that had become his world. But the cattails, the one moss-covered log that lay in a few inches of dark water, and the familiar, dank odor seemed to have lost their power to comfort him.

Now, he wanted more, and he wanted to know what this mouse knew. He wanted to know how a mouse got to be so, so...cocky. He wanted to get more than his head out of his shell. He wanted to stretch his arms and legs. He wanted to wear a tee shirt.

As his head and shoulders moved beyond the edge of his shell into daylight, he heard that tiny voice once more.

"Come on, big guy!" encouraged Ronald. "You're almost out! Just keep on breathing!"

Simon did, squirming, pushing, stretching, all the while aware of those inside feelings. Fear and excitement tumbled together in his belly and his chest. With his arms outside the shell, he grabbed the edges of his home, gave one last push and found himself naked, sprawled on the moist soil of the marsh, feeling for the first time the glorious warmth of the sun on his back and shoulders. For the moment, all he noticed were the feelings of excitement and joy that grew and spread through his entire body. He had left home at last!

"What now, big guy?" asked Ronald.

And with that question, the fear resurfaced in Simon's stomach. He didn't have a clue. Not a single thought, but there was something inside his head. There were pictures. Pictures he would draw and paint, pictures of himself carrying the perfect pencil over his shoulder, pictures of smiles on the faces of the mice, the snakes, the frogs, the birds who lived in the marsh and who would come to see Simon's drawings of the beautiful things that had always existed there.

Simon struggled to his feet, feeling exposed, and actually towering over the tiny, mighty mouse.

"I need a shirt," he said to Ronald.

Ronald pointed to a nearby willow, and hanging from the lowest branch, held up by two squirrels, was a t-shirt that said, "Big Guy." Simon, now standing, tried out this walking upright thing. More feelings arose in his body, as he toddled over to the shirt, took it from the squirrel paws, and pulled it over his head. Simon was officially out.

"What do I do now?" he asked Ronald.

"That's up to you," came the reply. "What makes your boat float?"

"I keep on seeing these pictures in my head, and I want to paint them, so everyone really sees how cool this swamp is. But I'm nervous. Real nervous."

"About what?" asked the mouse, looking up at Simon.

"About my mom. What's she going to say if she catches me out of my shell?"

"Don't know," answered Simon. "But what's the worst thing she could say?"

"Well, she'd yell at me, tell me I'm bad or crazy or both for leaving my shell."

"Is that the worst?"

"Well, not really. Then she'd probably start crying. I hate it when she does that. Just hate it!"

"How come?"

"Well, I just start to feel really bad. You know, like...like real guilty. Like I'm some slug, not a turtle anymore."

Ronald was thinking hard. His whiskers twitched, his small, black nose turned up a bit, his eyes squinted. Then he got it, by George. He got it!

"Listen, big guy, are you trying to hurt your mom's feelings?"

"No," Simon answered.

"Is there any rule that says that you have to stay in your shell forever and give up your dreams?"

Simon gave this one some thought. He had never looked at all of this in terms of unspoken rules.

"Guess not," he replied.

"Then where do all these ideas of 'bad or crazy or both' come from?"

"Uh, from my mom, I guess."

At this point, Ronald was poised at the height of logical brilliance. With an upward flip of his head, he folded his arms, drew himself up to his full mousy stature, and proclaimed, "Then you'll just have to leave them in your mom's head, where they belong or else you'll never draw a line or paint a picture. Ever."

*****

The last of the four steps in emotional mastery can be optional. It's the decision to act or not, to express or not. It is also the step that is commonly feared the most, because it invites us to interact with the world and with others. It's the arena in which we just might get hurt.

Recall the reasons we have feelings. They are our radar, and they connect us to others. They are also energizers and motivators, mobilizing us to do what has to be done and to express what has to be expressed. They let us know what is okay or not okay, then they motivate us to make things right when they're not.

Jeff, a fairly passive guy, never let himself show anger. Consequently, since no one ever knew when they were offending or violating him, he became a doormat. He had been struggling to regain visitation rights with his children, who lived with his former wife, a bitter and manipulative woman. Jeff never really let his anger show. He was too busy being afraid of his former wife's outbursts.

I received a call one day from the law guardian for the children, who was trying to arrange visitations that would be best for the children. She was concerned with Jeff's "anger management" problem.

I asked what she was referring to. As I later learned from Jeff, the law guardian had grilled him, asking him why he had been absent for so long from the children's lives. Jeff had been blocked every step of the way by his former wife in every attempt to have contact with his children. She seemed to care more about revenge than the children's well-being, and he had had it with the cumbersome legal system. As he told me over the phone, he felt manipulated and set up by the lawyer, so he got angry. Damned angry.

When I spoke with the law guardian over the phone, I realized that the lawyer's behavior was probably triggering memories of his ex-wife's strategies. I said, "Frankly, you've accomplished what I haven't been able to for a year! I think it's high time and that it's healthy that Jeff get angry. Without that anger, he'll probably give up on his kids."

It's one thing to feel anger. It's another thing to act appropriately, motivated by that feeling. This is different from angry behaviors that hurt others, the definition of aggression. An appropriate anger response sometimes goes by the name "righteous anger" or "justifiable anger." A critical difference between aggression and healthy anger is that in one, *we* have the anger. In the other, the anger has *us*.

Recently, during an NBA basketball game, players from the Detroit Pistons climbed into the stands and began to pummel a taunting fan. It is one thing to feel anger at being taunted and then use the anger to lift the quality of your play and/or to enlist the game officials in having raucous fans ejected. It's another thing to let the anger take over and beat up on fans. Bad decision, buzzer goes off, bad dog. You're grounded for the rest of the season.

Guilt is another example of a feeling that necessarily motivates us to act or speak. When we've hurt someone (having checked out the reality of that perception), it is quite fitting, as part of repairing our connection to that person (at-one-ment), to apologize. Without guilt, we're not motivated to do anything about the situation. We don't feel responsible to make amends. We move in the direction of the antisocial and the sociopath.

In medieval times, knights were trained in the art of war. If they ever used their skills to hurt or kill innocent people, their guilty behaviors demanded atonement. Particularly if they killed someone, unable to undo what they had done, the knight would be sent to a priest or monk, who in turn would mete out a penance.

Since neither undoing the deed nor relieving the negative weight from the moral scale were possibilities, the priest would assign the knight some task that would eventually balance the effects of the misdeed. The warrior might, for example, be asked to guard the commercial roads for several years, protecting travelers from thieves and bandits.

Drug dealers whose behaviors have resulted in the deaths of many teenagers in urban ghettos, when motivated by a healthy sense of guilt, commit themselves after their prison release to working with children and adolescents in crime-ridden areas of major cities. Without guilt, there would be no repairing of the societal tapestry. No return to community. And the guilt would persist until the work of atonement was undertaken.

It is important to recall that Steps One (awareness of the feeling) and Two (being with the feeling) are often sufficient for the return to internal equilibrium. The opposite of emotional repression or suppression, as mentioned earlier, is not expression. It is awareness. Regardless of how many of the four steps we employ, the return to an inner peace and balance, as well as to a healthy connection with our interpersonal world, are the goals of emotional mastery.

It is necessary to listen to and, eventually, trust our emotional guidance system to let us know whether emotional awareness and presence are enough, or whether action/expression is being called for. Only the individual can tell, moment to moment, event by event.

Ultimately, you need to ask yourself, "Am I doing (or not doing) this out of love or fear?" If it is out of love and consistent feelings of well-being (happy, excited, etc.), you are on the right road. If out of fear, you're heading down the wrong pike.

Simon could have stayed in his shell, but it would have been out of fear of the unknown, as well as fear of the world (including his mother). Sometimes the feeling, particularly fear (as in panic/anxiety) can be overwhelming, and we have to remember to enlist awareness and recognition (Step One), then breath and body relaxation (Step Two) to get us out of the fight/flight/freeze mode. Finally, we have to check out the messages, thoughts, and beliefs that go with the emotion.

When Simon finally made the decision to move out of his shell (comfort zone), he felt both the fear, which Ronald helped him assess, as well as the excitement, the positive motivator to move ahead and to "follow his bliss."

Simon was having a "desert experience." Just as the Israelites found themselves wandering around the desert, somewhere between the land of bondage (Egypt) and the promised land, Simon was caught between the familiar (but no longer satisfying) and a vision that both *scared the life out* of him and *jump-started his aliveness.* To submit to the fear without challenging it would be to die slowly inside his shell. To be moved to action by excitement was to give birth to a bigger world, and this included the birth pains of fear, guilt, sadness.

Would Simon be held hostage by fear or freed by love?

Goals of Emotional Mastery

- **To re-establish internal equilibrium and**

- **To clarify and repair our interpersonal web**

- **Based on love and not fear**

*****

73

A light began to creep across Simon's face, a glint in his eyes. He and Ronald were facing each other in a small clearing, savoring the moment, when the cattails and grasses around them parted slowly. Ronald heard the movement, turned, horrified to see Simon's mother, shell and all, entering the clearing looking shocked and angry.

"Simon! Simon Turtle!! What have you done!?! Cover yourself up right now!" she shrieked.

Simon froze. Ronald deflated a bit. There they were, Mighty Mouse and Big Guy, caught by the Ultimate Enforcer.

"Uh, uh...well, uh...," Simon stuttered.

"Speak up!" his mom demanded, a mix of fury and fear on her face. "What's become of you? What will the other turtles think?"

Simon's brain had gone offline. He couldn't think, speak, or even see straight. Everything around him blurred. All he could see was his mother's face and that look...the look that could penetrate the biggest rock or the widest tree trunk.

Then he felt a nudge from behind. In his panic, he had forgotten that Ronald was still there, gathering his own wits.

"Breathe! Remember? Breathe!"

Simon listened to the small voice and began to breathe. His vision began to widen just a bit.

"Relax your shoulders."

Simon wasn't even aware that his shoulders were touching his ears. He was as tense as a board all over. He followed the instructions and began to notice his brain clearing and words beginning to form in his head.

"Uh, uh, mom, I just gotta do this…"

Now it was mostly fear that sat heavily on his mother's face.

"But Simon, it's so dangerous out there…and all that I've taught you…"

Simon could feel heat creep across his face. It felt as if he was ruining everything for everyone.

"Go, big guy! You're on a roll," whispered Ronald.

Simon breathed again.

"Mom, I know, I know it can be hard outside the shell and outside our part of the swamp," Simon said, "but I'm just not happy there anymore. I'm scared, but I'm excited, too, for the first time in my life. And I'm making new friends!"

"You mean that rodent?!" his mother snapped.

Ronald winced, but knew enough to stay out of the conversation.

"Mom, he's been a great friend. He's been teaching me how to take care of myself in the open swamp…just like you taught me to take care of myself inside my shell and in our part of the swamp.

"Smooth move!" Ronald noted to himself.

"I've got to make pictures for others to see. What do you say, Mom? I'll make the first one for you!"

"Oh, this guy's good!" Ronald thought.

Simon's mother was softening. She was clearly nervous, very nervous, but beginning to realize she couldn't control her son's life the way she used to.

"If I might add something, ma'am?" ventured Ronald.

"Squeak up, I can't hear you!" said Simon's mom, just a bit sarcastically. After all, she had to blame someone...

Covering up his annoyance, Ronald said, "I'd be nervous, too, if it were my son. But it's like a bird in a nest. If the momma bird keeps the baby safe in the nest, the young one never learns to fly."

Simon's mother was impressed. This mouse had more behind his whiskers than his nose.

"Hm-m-m-m," she murmured, finding her own feelings quieting down, finding her thoughts heading down different channels. "You might have a point. But he might get hurt!"

Yes, ma'am," replied Ronald. "But with all of his new friends and with you to check in with him each day," he looked over at Simon, who flinched a tad, "he might get hurt from time to time, but we'll help him up, he'll just get stronger, and then he gets to paint the world in pictures. That will be so amazing...and it will be your son doing all that!"

They all grew quiet in the clearing. Visions of possibilities arose among them wordlessly. The sun was beginning to retreat, as the swamp slipped into its evening silence.

The world was becoming bigger. Their hearts were beating a bit faster as they felt the fears and the excitement. They also felt something unusual, something none of them had a word for. But they felt it in their throats and just *behind their eyes. It had something to do with being in that clearing together and leaving old ways behind. It had to do with the sun warming them, marshy paths inviting them. It had to do with being together and part of something larger than they had ever imagined.*

*****

And so our hero, listening to his emotional guidance system, checking it out when necessary, supported by the wisdom of a mouse, motivated by his own sense of excitement, enters life itself.

This is what our feelings are there to help us do--to move more and more fully into aliveness, into active living in accordance with the best in each of us. Nothing less.

Step Four, as mentioned earlier, is a choice point. To do, or not to do. To express, or not to express. To intend and to act--or not act--in accordance with the best in us is, in fact, to act out of love rather than fear.

Simon experienced several feelings back to back, an emotional flooding that is fairly common. He got to the feeling that supported his best by allowing one feeling at a time, finally deciding to act upon the excitement rather than the fear and guilt. If he had acted upon the fear, he would have returned to his shell. If guilt held forth, he would have stayed with his mother, rather than upset the familiar system of life as they had known it.

In either case, staying with fear or guilt would have supported the immediate gain of avoiding the excitement, bypassing the need for the courage to act and move forward. Instead of being stuck on the first or second wave of emotion, Simon tolerated them, moved through them, and experienced the emotion that emanated from the best in him. This is a phenomenon I call *emotional layering*, a topic for a later chapter. As we follow one feeling after another organically, we eventually reach a place of equilibrium and satisfaction. If we *avoid or get attached to* any one feeling, we remain stuck in emotional mud, spinning our wheels, wondering why we so often return to (or never leave) the same spot.

Ronald, on the other hand, had to decide *not* to act upon his feelings. Anger arose when Simon's mother insulted him. He might have gotten hot, insulted Simon's mother, and made things much worse. He could have spoken up for himself appropriately, motivated by the anger, but that wouldn't have created the optimal outcome, and might have caused his early death! Instead, he recognized and breathed into the anger, breathed it out, and decided to let it go in the service of a more beneficial moment that came later, when he shared his wisdom with Simon's mother.

Simon's mother went through her own emotional layering, from fury, anger, irrational fear, and, finally, to a rational fear of the possibility of Simon getting hurt. She, too, chose not to act out of fear. It would have been different if her fear were due to Simon doing something really stupid and dangerous. But she was confronted with an existential fear, one that is part and parcel of living in a world that is often unpredictable and unknowable. She noticed her emotions, but allowed her brain and Ronald's input to balance the feelings, leading her to a larger view of things.

Step Four often provides us with the opportunity to marry a clear mind with an open heart. When called for, rather than demanded by some "should," this internal marriage creates a palpable sense of efficacy, competence, and security in an often unpredictable and, sometimes, hostile world.

It is interesting that avoiding feelings and the action they might call for is often driven by a fantasy of safety and hope. "If I keep quiet, I'll be okay." The irony is that the opposite occurs. We sink more and more into a life of fearful avoidance that never feels secure or creates authentic safety. True security is an inside job.

Step Four - Summary

- To act or express the feeling is a *decision or choice.*

- The choice should be based on *love, not fear.*

- When several feelings occur (*layering*), follow one after the other until you rest in the feeling that calls you clearly to action/expression.

- Remember the importance of clear thought supporting emotional response – the marriage of mind and heart.

Which decision to make when fear, guilt, anger, or excitement arise is not difficult much of the time. Yet, at other times, as in Ronald's case, we have to weigh the merit of our various options.

This becomes a bit more difficult when the decision we face has more to do with possible *expression*, rather than some other action.

Veronica became angry with her husband, Dick, on a regular basis. Dick would often buy new tools for himself, even a new truck at one point. Anything that was purchased for Veronica was second-hand, whether it was her stove, refrigerator or her car. She felt second-class, but never voiced her anger and hurt. Consequently, nothing changed.

I asked if she might be interested in finding her voice and being able to express her frustrations and desires.

"Why bother?" she said. "Nothing will change. He'll just blow me off, and I'll just get more aggravated!"

There were two things that Veronica didn't understand. First, to express an emotion to someone else is *its own reward.* If the other responds positively, that's gravy. When expressed, the feeling no longer hangs like dead weight around your heart or your gut. You honor your own emotions and, in so doing, yourself. Withheld feelings grow heavier with time. It is not unlike holding up a one-pound bag of sugar in front of you. In the beginning, it feels like one pound. As you continue to hold the sugar up, it gets heavier and heavier.

A feeling is *emotion*, needing to move through and out. When it is in need of expression and the expression occurs, there is typically an experience of relief, lightness and, increased positive energy. This is your system's signal that you did what was needed. You acted out of love, not fear—whether fear of hurting the other, fear of reactions, fear of loss of love or approval. That leads us to the second point that Veronica was missing.

When our system calls for expression, it is leading us to *greater contact and connection with the other.* Even if Dick were to respond negatively to Veronica's complaint, Veronica would feel more connected to herself, thus opening the possibility for more connection to Dick as well. Even in disagreement and anger, we can still connect to each other if we are truthful and responsible (that is, not blaming, attacking, or defending) in how we express our feelings. The A.R.T. of emotional truth-telling is discussed in Chapter 12.

The more Veronica withholds her emotions, including her anger, the heavier her emotional weight becomes, the more disempowered she experiences herself, and the more distant she feels from Dick. Internally, she blames him for all of that, but she is as much a part of the problem as he.

Radical honesty is not always easy, but this is not about feeling "good" all the time. It's more about the increase of positive energy and a felt sense of connection. At times, we have to go through unpleasant confrontation and conflict to get there, but the price is well worth it.

It's Time to Act/Express...

- **When the action/expression isn't dangerous (and it usually isn't).**

- **When feeling the weight of inaction or withheld feelings and in need of more positive energy.**

- When feeling powerless, weak, voiceless.

- When feeling the disconnect from another due to inaction or withheld feelings and in need of renewed contact or connection.

- When holding someone else responsible for your own misery or happiness.

Spend this next week focusing on increasing your awareness of emotional moments and whether they are calling for action and/or expression. You're still in training; remember that the journey of becoming an emotional expert requires courage, consistency, and gratitude for the feelings that work for you, for the mind that balances them, and for the love that is just waiting to move them and yourself into aliveness.

Practice

1. Remember to apply the first three steps to emotional events, and then

2. Jot down or journal about what you experienced and learned from the feeling.

3. In each event, apply Step Four by asking, "Is there any action or expression being called for here?"

4. If the answer is no, you're done. Just be with the feeling until it passes.

5. If the answer is yes, check out the behavioral options, decide which to pursue (based on love, not fear), and do it.

6. Jot or journal. Also note how you felt (energy and connection) afterwards.

7. If you find you're not able to follow through, accept that (awareness without judgment) and learn what you can by asking, "What am I afraid of?" or "What am I managing to avoid by not acting or expressing?" "What do I need (internal resources, skills, knowledge) to do this differently next time?"

8. Jot or journal.

9. Continue to repeat the previous steps for the rest of your life.

PART THREE

Refining Emotional Competence

Chapter 7:

Avoiding, Burying and Other Survival Strategies

Not much time had passed since Simon had announced his new way of life to his mother. He began to find favorite spots in the swamp where he would set up his easel and paintbrushes. Occasionally, however, he would pass by his old chomping grounds and his abandoned shell. Often enough, he would spy his mother lying there, her head hanging out of her shell, with that same look.

"*I just* hate *that look!" he told Ronald one cloudy morning.*

"*What look?" asked the mouse.*

"*The angry one! Like she's not going to forgive me, no matter what, for leaving my shell."*

"*And...?" prodded Ronald.*

"*And then I feel sort of bad," Simon replied.*

"*Bad?"*

"*Well, you know, guilty. I push it away for a while, but it always comes back, and then I feel worse."*

"*Okay, okay, review lesson number one," stated Ronald. "Did you violate your mother? Break any agreement?"*

"*No," replied Simon.*

"*Alright, then we have a false alarm. And what set the alarm off?" asked Ronald.*

"I told you, it's the look!" answered Simon impatiently.

"A look is a look until you put a story to it. What's your story?" asked Ronald.

"That she's mad because I left," came the reply.

"And where does the story come from?" asked Ronald, drawing himself up once again, as he closed in for the big question.

"From her?"

"You don't know that, do you?"

"From me?"

"Maybe. Only one way to find out, isn't there?"

After the full impact of Ronald's questioning sank in, Simon made his way through the reeds, around weathered logs, to the place where his mother would typically be resting. He found her taking in the sun in a small clearing by the water's edge. She lifted her head, somewhat surprised, still with that look.

"Mom," Simon stammered, "I... I need to clear something up with you."

"What's that?" she replied. "You've made your decision."

With that statement, his guilt resurrected.

"Well, you look so angry. Are you?"

"I was, but not anymore."

"But that look...!" he said.

"Oh, I've always had that look. Even as a baby turtle, my mother said I frowned all the time. Like I had swallowed a spider or something."

"So you're not angry?" Simon asked.

"No, no. I think I'm over that. But I think I get that ~ook when anything bothers me. And right now, I guess I'm just afraid. Afraid that you'll get hurt..."

"Oh," muttered Simon, as his story and his guilt faded.

*****

Basic Strategies

Growing up, we rarely received coaching or education regarding our feelings. It was up to us to figure out how to navigate the emotional waters of childhood. Since we couldn't handle feelings, we learned various ways to ignore and deny their existence.

To whatever extent we made it through, to that extent we must be grateful for our survival instincts. The problem, however, is that as adults, we still use the survival strategies developed during our early years. We ignore and deny, believing on some level that this will keep us safe and sort of happy, just as it did when we were much younger.

But the strategies that kept us intact as children now prevent us from entering into healthy relationships as adults. We want freedom from emotional pain, but don't realize that freedom only arrives with our willingness to stop trying to escape from our feelings. We live in an adult world in an adult body, but emotionally we act like kids.

Mary Jane grew up in a house in which only her father's voice and opinions counted. Only her father could display anger. Her younger sister had suffered with cerebral palsy since birth and demanded most of her parents' attention and energy. Mary Jane had to be the perfect child. Her parents had enough to deal with.

She learned early on not to let herself feel anger. She had a sense that it wasn't right. More importantly, it wasn't safe, given her father's volcanic eruptions and her mother's helplessness when he exploded. And it certainly wasn't okay to be resentful towards her sister. "Look at the deck *she* had been dealt," she would think.

Mary Jane learned to ignore any feelings of anger. She wouldn't let the body sensations or the angry thoughts enter her awareness. Most of the time, consequently, they didn't even exist. Mary Jane had developed ***avoiding*** into an art form, and, for the most part, it worked.

There were times, however, when her anger at feeling invisible and neglected would slip by the sentry and creep into her consciousness. As soon as she noticed the feeling, she would push it back behind a protective wall. She learned that ***burying*** her anger was a good backup when avoiding wasn't enough. Sometimes the burying happened automatically (repression); sometimes she had to do it intentionally (suppression).

Mary Jane made it through childhood this way, but unfortunately married a man just like her father: a bully and a dictator who was not much fun to be with. Now, as a married woman, she would clean the house furiously when her anger arose, particularly when, after their first child was born, her husband forbade her to have a second. The cleaning helped her avoid her feelings by distracting her and keeping the anger out of her awareness. After all, this is what she had learned all those years growing up.

Sometimes the cleaning wasn't enough, so she stopped eating. At least she had control over her food. She almost killed herself. Her body became little more than a skeleton with a thin veil of skin. It was at this point that she was referred to my office.

As she sat in front of me in my office, telling me of her husband's refusal to have another child, her jaw clenched and her fists tightened. When I asked her what she might be feeling, she replied, "Oh, nothing."

I drew attention to her jaw and fists, and tried the multiple-choice approach. "Any anger?" I asked.

"No, not at all!" she responded sincerely.

Mary Jane had avoided and buried all her anger. She had virtually eliminated it from consciousness. She had won the immediate battle of not feeling, but lost the war of reclaiming her voice and making herself count. Her childhood strategies kept her from receiving the guidance and the support of her adult anger.

Avoiding emotions keeps them out of awareness so that we don't have to deal with them at all. Burying them squelches the first signs of a feeling that is unwanted and often feared. We fear them because having them does not feel safe, because we don't think we can deal with them, or because we fear we might have to do something about them. Avoiding is remedied with attention to Step One: Awareness of the feeling. Burying requires the courage of Step Two: Having the feeling.

Being aware of and having her anger and hurt was the healthier alternative for Mary Jane. Even if she had not been ready to confront her father or husband, she would have had the satisfaction of honoring her emotions and releasing them, either alone, in her journal, or to a friend. Chances are she wouldn't have to clean her house as often or starve herself as severely. Healthy emotional control results from Steps One and Two. Fear-based emotional control can kill you.

More Basic Strategies: Generalizing, Cognizing, Blaming and Masking

Even when we are in touch with an emotion, we often dilute or disguise the expression of it, leaving others with only a vague sense of how we are feeling. We *generalize* when, instead of communicating a specific emotional reaction when asked how we are, we say things like, "I'm feeling *bad*," or "I'm *upset*," rather than *hurt* or *angry*. For positive responses, we often say, "I'm *fine*" or "*good*," rather than *happy, excited, or calm* (see Chapter Four for the list of feelings).

Another common strategy that keeps us away from our emotional truth is *cognizing*, which we do when we substitute a thought for a feeling. "I feel that you're treating me unfairly" is a description of a thought, perception or an idea, *not* an emotion, even though we use the words "I feel" (instead of "I think" or "I believe"). To bring in the emotion, we would say something like, "When I *think* I'm being treated unfairly, I *feel* angry (or hurt, scared, etc.)."

Blaming is simply that: blaming someone else for "*making*" *us* feel something. This is a disempowering statement, since it attributes to someone else the power to control your feelings. No one makes us feel anything. You react the way you do because of your individual history and unique personality composition. Someone else might react with a different feeling or not react at all.

When we take responsibility for our emotional reactions, we are able to learn from them. This is a more powerful position than putting someone else in the driver's seat of our emotional van. When we give someone else our power by blaming them, we eliminate the possibility of learning and making choices for ourselves. We have placed ourselves in a victim's position, a position of no choice, no efficacy. Blaming will be revisited in Chapter 10.

Notice the difference between blaming and claiming responsibility. A wife may complain to her husband: "You make me so angry! When are you going to learn to be on time? Don't you think I deserve better?!?" Compare that with, "I get so angry when you keep coming home late, because I deserve better." The shift is from the second-person (you) blaming to the first-person (I) taking responsibility for making her feelings and her desires known to her husband.

Graduate Level Strategies...Dumping, Masking and Projecting

Keith's really grown to dislike his job, but he doesn't pay much attention to his feelings of dissatisfaction. They would cause too much grief. His boss is a pain: critical, unreasonable, and demanding. He really pisses Keith off, but

Keith won't speak up. He believes he can't afford to lose the job he dislikes so much. He's not a happy camper.

Keith returns home, still carrying anger ("It's not fair!"), a sense of helplessness ("Nothing I can do about it!") and shame ("I'm never good enough"). No sooner is one foot inside the door than he bellows at his wife, Sarah, "Why the hell are these toys all over the living room? And someone turn off that damned music!!"

Sarah, having dealt all day with a child in diapers running around as if permanently on high-test and a melodramatic adolescent daughter, is trying to cook supper. At Keith's belligerent entry, her frustration and hurt spike, but she dares not say anything, given Keith's mood. So she does what comes naturally--she screams at Kim, their daughter.

Kim, not having a clue why her mom just went off on her, turns around and screams at the dog. Bodkins, their golden retriever, usually a black hole for attention, is totally befuddled, and does what is natural for a canine. He goes after Phoebe, the cat.

Phoebe has nowhere to go, nowhere to dump her feelings, so she pees on the rug. This in turn sets off Keith, so the family pattern repeats again and again.

Dumping is aiming the expression of our feelings in the wrong place. We're aware of them and have them, but are not willing to express them to the appropriate person or in the appropriate situation. They build up, and without realizing it, we express the anger or irritation, in this case, toward the wrong person or animal.

Often we don't even realize we are dumping. It's usually done out of a fear of repercussion. Unfortunately, the immediate gain in safety usually boomerangs, creates more stress due to the emotional stockpiling, and damages other relationships.

The alternative would be to tell the emotional truth to the right person. Keith needs to speak with his boss, Sarah with her husband, Kim with her mother. Bodkins and Phoebe will be fine as soon as the humans begin to tell each other the truth, something we will look at more closely in Chapter 10.

It may be scary for Keith to speak to his boss, but how long has he been holding back, and what effect has it had on his physical well-being and his family life? The same is true for Sarah and Kim. The courage to feel is required to set things straight and to create a more satisfying work and family atmosphere. There is no other way out of our relational looping and repetition than through "radical honesty." Frightening at first, but freeing and corrective in the end, attention to Steps Three (Checking the Message) and Four (Expressing, Acting) breaks the unhealthy pattern.

Masking is the Colgate-smile approach to emotional deception. We cover one "dangerous," feared feeling with another that we believe we can tolerate more easily or that will be more acceptable to others. Emily, not wanting to "bother" her friends by "dumping" on them, would inevitably respond with a broad smile and "Fine!" when asked if her recent bout with depression had lifted. When angry at her husband, David, for not even asking her how she was doing, she simply looked sad and began to tear up in front of him. It was safer to appear sad, rather than angry.

David, on the other hand, was only able to show two emotions: happy and angry (commonly dubbed "glad and mad"). It's a guy thing. When afraid for his wife and her depression, when anxious about his teenage daughter on her first date, he became irritable and angry, unable to reveal the "softer" emotions of fear, jealousy and sadness.

As with other strategies to keep us from feeling and revealing what is happening inside our emotional world, masking disconnects us from ourselves and from those around us. It prevents our authentic feelings from being resolved and, instead, creates a stockpile of irritation that becomes angry outbursts ("What's his problem?"), sadness that becomes depression ("Why can't she just get over it?") and fear that settles into an ongoing anxiety ("What's the big deal?"). Our Four Steps provide the strategy that can reverse this process.

Projecting shows how clever we can be in our need to avoid our own feeling responses. Have you ever walked into a room of people you don't know, convinced at first glance that everyone (or at least that classy-looking woman across the room) is judging you? Or certain that the party host is angry? Or that the person sitting by himself on the couch is desperately sad? The judging, the anger, and the sadness come from a story you are telling yourself. That story, and the feelings that go with it, were created by you.

Let's imagine that you have an inadequate sense of yourself in social situations where you don't know many people. You enter the party, and, rather than taking responsibility (the ability to respond) for your own self-criticism, particularly if you're not even aware of a sense of inadequacy building up, you imagine it coming from others. The major drawback is that you make others out to be worse than they are, you don't challenge the source of the criticism that makes you out to be less than you are, and you wind up having a miserable time

Is the party host angry? Or am I angry for having to be at this damned party at all? Why didn't I speak up to my partner? Why does it always have to be his way? And as for that poor wretch sitting by himself on the couch, I can't imagine ever feeling all right about myself sitting alone. Especially at a party! And what would people think of me if I were sitting by myself? So who's the sad one?

The world is often a projection screen for our unwanted feelings, with the original movie and its projector inside our head. Instead of being aware of and claiming our own emotional responses, we imagine them to be someone else's, since that's safer. Projection, in a word, is attributing to someone else what belongs to us.

Projection disowns that which belongs to us: our feelings, what we dislike and even what we like about our self. Because the distorted lens of our projections is so convincing, we are certain that what we see is the way it is out there.

A helpful way to determine the presence of projection is, first of all, to do a reality check of the situation by asking the other if she/he is angry, sad or whatever. If that's not an option, then at least be aware of the story you are telling yourself about the other and remember that it may be wrapped around something that might belong to you.

Finally, use your awareness to see if anything of what you perceive in others is active within yourself.

It is interesting how we project even our positive feelings and qualities onto others. Joyce was an extremely creative person, which showed in the way she decorated her home, the way she dressed, and the time she spent attending performances and exhibitions of local artists. Yet her common reaction to artistic people was, "God, you creative people are so lucky! I just wish I were like that." The reality was that she not only saw creativity in others, but disowned her own, afraid of it and how she might have to step into a different kind of life if she owned her own talents. Projecting her creativity and the excitement that accompanied it onto others was safer. (An excellent book about projection is Debbie Ford's, *The Dark Side of the Light Chasers.*)

Why bother being so clear about and responsible for what we are feeling? Getting to the heart of what we are experiencing emotionally lets us know where we stand in relationship to ourselves, others, and the world around us. The more we fine-tune the emotional radar screen, the more empowered we are to live a life of choice.

TRAINING

1. Notice when you use any of the survival strategies mentioned in this chapter: avoiding, burying, generalizing, cognizing, masking or projecting. Write it down!

2. From which feeling(s) did it protect you?

3. What was the feeling trying to tell you before you dismissed it?

4. Note the fears or the payoff that motivated you to *not* deal with the emotion.

5. What is the worst thing that might happen if you expressed or acted? What would be the best-case scenario (think integrity, relief, connection)?

6. Where did you first learn this strategy? Did it work then? Is it working now?

Chapter 8:

Layering

Ronald peered over Simon's shoulder one morning as the turtle painted away. What Ronald saw on the canvas resembled nothing he had ever seen in the swamp. Thick layers of reds and blacks, swirling and diving into each other.

"Bad hair day?" quipped the mouse.

"Not funny, not funny at all," answered Simon.

"Sorry, big guy. No offense. What's going on? I've never seen anything like that before."

"Oh, I'm just grumpy, irritated, frustrated. Not sure why, but that's what it feels like," he said, pointing to the canvas.

Ronald thought for a moment, then ventured, "Is this more mom stuff?"

"Yeah, I think so. When I think of her being scared and all, I just get angry. Don't know why. I mean, she's not hurting me or anything like that."

"Why don't we just hang out with that red and black stuff and see what happens?" suggested Ronald. "It's like asking if there's anything else there, maybe underneath the reds and blacks. Then you just wait for the answer."

And so a bit of time passed, as Simon sat in front of his feelings, and images of his frightened mother with "that look" passed through his head.

"Hm-m-m," muttered Simon. "It's not as strong now."

"You mean the irritation?"

"Yeah. It's not as strong. Funny, but it just sort of feels sad. I think I need different colors."

*****

Our emotional system is set up in a way that allows us to move naturally from less to more difficult feelings. This works well as long as we are conscious and aware of this pattern. If not, we are liable to remain fixed on our initial feelings, rather than progress to the deeper emotional messages. In men, for example, anger can cover fear/anxiety that might sit on top of guilt or grief, which might muffle a deep-seated shame. Women often lead with sadness or anxiety, which might well cover hurt, anger, or shame.

Steven was not your typical male. He tended to be quite outgoing and social and was typically comfortable with most of his emotions. I was surprised to receive a call from him one day, asking to come in.

As he sat across from me, his face tightened and his eyes narrowed.

"I'm pissed off at my dad, and I feel crummy about that!"

"What's going on?" I asked.

"Well, he's just deteriorating! You know, can't get around much, forgets things, and now it's getting to the point where he has to be fed specially ground up food. And then he totally loses it and messes his pants. Damn, it's like having to take care of a kid!"

Steven spent the next quarter of an hour venting both his anger and his guilt about the anger. He then told me the story of how his father used to be so healthy, alive, and outgoing, just as Steven was.

"And I remember the time," he continued, "when I was a kid, around ten or eleven. I was in the Little League and got myself into a batting slump. So my dad would go out to the ball field with me, and work to help me out of my slump."

Steven's face was softening a bit as he recalled that moment.

"And so I got over that slump because he was there for me."

"And can you," I asked, "help him out of *his* slump?"

The painful answer was all too obvious. Tears flowed, as Steven went below the anger and guilt to the depths of his profound helplessness and grief. This is layering.

Stacey, on the other hand, never knew her own anger. It sat behind tears and fears. As a child, she had witnessed her father lift her mother by the throat and smash her back against the wall. Her mother hadn't walked straight since. No one in the family besides the father could ever get angry. If anyone stepped out of line to express any form of frustration, they were backhanded or terrified by the sheer force of his verbal rage. It wasn't worth the risk.

In our work together, it took time to move through the layers that sat on top of her rage. At the very mention of her father, she would break into tears. "It's so sad!" she would murmur. She would return to the sadness over and over, quickly moving away from it by changing the subject. Nothing changed.

Eventually during one session, she dared to stay with the sadness long enough to go beyond it in order to see what else might be calling for attention. As the sadness subsided, she recognized the presence of anxiety and fear in her stomach. Again, she faced the temptation of moving away from the energy of the new feelings, but stayed with it instead. The anxiety finally subsided, as all feelings do if we stay present to them.

What followed caught both of us a bit off guard. Stacey, a well-contained church-going woman, straightened up from her protective ball posture on the couch, got what seemed like an adrenaline overdose, and spurted:

"That goddamn, spineless sonovaBITCH!"

Her anger shot from beneath her grief and fear, straightened her spine, energized her, and allowed her to see her father as a bully and herself, finally, as a grown, empowered woman.

Layering is a term I use to describe the frequent way in which one feeling often hides behind, or is buried under, another. It's not a strategy that we consciously or semi-consciously employ to disconnect from our emotional system as we saw in the previous chapter, yet it is inherent in our discomfort with certain feelings. It's the way our feelings sometimes surface one after the other in layers, allowing us to move in a gradual manner through the various emotions connected to a specific event.

During the early years of our marriage, with five children between us, Barb and I would regularly set off one of our mutual triggers. It would go something like this:

Barb: I don't know how we're going to pay for everything with all the kids, and then go on a vacation, too!"

Andrew: But didn't we work out the numbers?

Barb: Yes, but everything just costs more and more.

Andrew: But we took that into account already. And I'm bringing in more income these days. So I don't get it! What's the problem?"

Barb: You don't understand. Your brain just doesn't think in those terms. You know, organizing future stuff.

Andrew: My brain works just fine! It's that damn anxiety of yours!

Barb: I'm not anxious. I'm *concerned*!

I wasn't able to get Barb to stop being "concerned," so I did what came naturally and simply got pissed off. After all, there was no reason to get anxious about the money stuff, and wasn't I bringing in enough? This was a mutual trigger in action: Barb's nervousness about finances triggering my "never good enough" theme, then my reactivity convincing her that I just wasn't hearing her or her concerns. My anger was the layer that protected me from having to face the shame-based experience of never feeling good enough.

I began to wonder why anger would come up for me when Barb became nervous about finances. Anger, as I recalled its message, had to do with *perceived or real* violation. How was she violating me? And with these questions in mind, I fell asleep one night, only to wake up for some reason around 3:00 A.M.

As I awoke, I noticed (Awareness) an electric sort of feeling pulsating across my stomach, a physical signal that I recognized as (oh, great surprise) anxiety. I sat up and began to breathe into it, wondering what the fear was about. Very soon, simply by keeping my awareness open, I began to notice several thoughts passing through my mind. "Will I always have to work this hard? Will there ever be enough? How do I deal with these insurance companies and managed care groups that do everything to avoid reimbursing me for sessions?"

It became clear that sitting underneath my anger towards Barb was my own anxiety about finances, and I just wasn't ready to face it until this moment. The anger was only the tip of the iceberg. Beneath the surface of the water lay my own fears, which I unconsciously didn't want to touch. As I sat with this awareness, another layer was revealed. There was a sense of inadequacy that I wasn't earning enough to allay the fears of the woman I call "my beloved." Shame lay at the bottom of it all.

As I described all of this to Barb the next morning, she released an enormous sigh of relief. Not only did she feel heard, but she no longer felt as if she was the only one who had to take on the responsibility for economic concern.

My emotional system had layered three feelings: anger, anxiety, and shame. My job was to be aware of whatever was on the surface and be with it until it either taught me what it had to teach or opened up to another level of emotion. Rather than blame Barb for "making me angry," it was time for me to take responsibility for my own feelings and to explore the beliefs that were triggering them. After becoming clear about my own fears and self-doubt (Steps One, Two and Three), it was time to tell this truth to Barb (Step 4). Simply put, the way out of our repeated argument was to uncover the feelings being experienced and to tell the truth about them.

If a feeling returns again and again, there's a good chance that one of three things is happening. One is that the feeling has not really been acknowledged and experienced (Steps One and Three) and is unfinished. The second occurs when a feeling is encouraging us toward some expression or action (Step Four), yet we continue to ignore its prompting. A repeated feeling can finally occur when layering is taking place, and the deeper feelings simultaneously are hidden by the repeated, surface emotion. The feelings being avoided in this third scenario effectively feed and drive the more apparent emotion.

What to do? The first strategy I recommend is *patience and presence*. Stay with the feeling that you are aware of, and if there is layering going on, the disguised emotions will surface once you are more comfortable with the original emotion. At this point, when the energy of the feeling quiets down, you can notice the emotion beneath it. When you ride or surf the wave of one emotion until it passes through, you will soon discover if there are deeper emotional currents to be experienced.

Another strategy for uncovering underlying emotions is one that I call *intuitive questioning*. You ask yourself a question, drop it into your awareness as if dropping a stone into a pond, then wait and watch to see what answers spontaneously arise, as ripples on a pond's surface.

A very useful intuitive question when you suspect layering (or avoiding, burying, denying, for that matter) is: *If I weren't feeling this feeling over and over, what else might I be experiencing or feeling?* Then wait to notice what you notice. This is what Simon did after Ronald encouraged him to ask what might lie beneath the reds and the blacks that Simon had painted.

If allowed, our innate guidance system will do what it is meant to do. It will facilitate healing. In our inner world, one thing always follows another, and if we attend to and allow the feelings to happen, we will naturally move towards a state of emotional equilibrium and balance.

Chapter 9:

Riding the Waves, Surviving the Desert

There were days when some of Simon's sadness about his mother still lingered, when his paintings didn't look that good to him, when he simply didn't know where his life was going. These were the hardest days of all.

All kinds of emotions would come crashing over him. In one moment, he was sad, then angry, then fearful, then bored, then nervous, then frustrated that he couldn't make sense of all the signals coming at him so quickly. He wondered if his radar was on the blink.

"What's going on?" he asked Ronald, who had stopped by on his way to one of the far ends of the swamp, a trip he made with some frequency. "All these feelings, and I just get more and more confused, then sort of nothing."

"Sometimes we just don't know. We can't go back to the way things were, and we don't know how or where to go forward. It's a hard place to be in. Like in the middle of nowhere."

"So, what do I do? I mean, have you ever had that problem? You always seem to know where you're going."

"Well, it wasn't always that way," replied Ronald.

"What do you mean?" asked Simon.

"Oh, that's a story for another time. The main thing that I learned was that you have to ride it out and trust that there's something on the other side of where you feel stuck or empty."

"Even though I don't have a clue about what's on the other side? That fox could be there! Nothing could be there!"

"Yep, that does make it scary," replied Ronald. "I used to think that I always had to know what to do, that I always had to do something. Not knowing what was next and not doing anything together felt like too much, so I just got busy. But that usually didn't work.

"I remember, in that big city up north where I got started, feeling real antsy and frustrated all the time. Then I'd get so bored. What I did then was to get busy, helping all kinds of mice out, especially the old ones, making a whole bunch of new mouse holes. Busy, busy, busy. But nothing changed until I stopped and let that irritation and boredom pass. It was kind of funny, totally new for me, but the quieter I got, the more I heard this voice in my head."

"You heard voices?" asked Simon.

"Actually, it wasn't like a real voice, but I somehow knew what the problem was. It just came to me. I knew I had to get out of the city."

"Is that how you got here?" asked Simon.

"It was the first step," replied Ronald. "Then all sorts of things happened, and eventually I met you!"

"Amazing," said Simon. "So, what do I do?"

"Not much," was the reply. "Let things pass, and listen for that voice."

*****

Emotions don't always arrive in neat streams. At times, depending on the intensity of our experience, feelings can land like a tsunami, one huge wave following the next, pounding against the shores of our awareness. This is when we need to ride the waves, one after the other, rather than try to dam them up.

The phone at our home office rang late one evening. I was close by, so I screened the call, looking forward to a relaxing evening, "No such luck," I thought, as I heard Natalie's anxious voice on the answering machine. I decided to pick it up.

"What's happening, Nat?"

"It's too much! Just too much! I don't know whether to shoot myself or kill the bitch!"

Not good options.

Natalie had struggled for most of her adult life with a severe mood disorder as well as a sense of self that was as fragile at times as Queen Anne's lace. She just didn't know how to deal with life.

"Nat, slow down. Breathe."

"It's the bitch I work for. It's never good enough. Never!"

"Can you slow down a bit more and tell me about it?"

"I can't!! I can't even put my thoughts together. It's too much. I'm so scared. Whacked out of control! And, god, this is so infuriating! And I want to kill the bitch!"

The storm had hit. Natalie had to somehow stay afloat, and not drown in the intensity of her hurt and anger. She had to manage her emotions and resist acting until the feelings subsided.

"What do I do?" she pleaded. "Tell me! What do I do now!?"

"Nothing! I said. "You're not supposed to do anything."

"Not even kill the miserable witch?"

"Nothing. It's like you're in a sailboat right now, Nat, in the middle of the ocean. In the middle of a storm. You've just got to take down the sails, point the boat into the wind, and hang on for dear life. Don't try to figure out directions or anything. Just breathe and hang on to the mast. Do you hear me?"

A pause followed. I could hear her begin to breathe.

"Okay. Okay....I'm breathing....okay."

"Watch it all. Okay, there's the fear, the sadness, the rage.....let them pass. It may take a few minutes, but it *will* pass."

And so it did. Natalie had survived an emotional storm.

These storms occur when someone or some event triggers our emotional sore spots. Imagine getting punched in the same spot on your arm repeatedly. All it takes, then, is for someone to tap you on that spot to get your attention, and you hit the roof. Your reaction towards that person's touch is intense, not because the touch was hard, but because you were *already* sore where you'd *already* been punched.

These sore places in our psyche are hangovers from past, typically painful, experiences that have not been resolved. They are over historically, but not experientially.

What makes these experiences painful are the emotions attached to them. Like radioactive material stored behind some neurological wall in our brain, they go off when triggered by any person or event that is in any way similar to the original experience. Natalie's parents, particularly her mother, were extremely demanding. Nothing she did was ever good enough. And so it seemed with her job supervisor who set off all of the unfinished emotional business from her past. Natalie's reaction was huge compared to the actual triggering event with her supervisor. The past was piggybacking on the present, making the present an overwhelming experience. In everyone's eyes, Natalie was just "too emotional." To Natalie, her somewhat critical supervisor deserved death by some slow and, preferably, supremely painful means.

The most important and critical step in the event of such a storm is to *recognize that you are in it*. Without this awareness, you are convinced that the way you are perceiving the present moment is actually the way it is. In point of fact, you are looking through that lens that is colored by your past experiences.

Then follows the task of riding out the storm, using the skills described in Chapter Four. In Natalie's case, this meant breathing and grounding herself in the present moment by keeping her eyes open, rather than going inward and getting caught up in the story she was creating about her supervisor.

Finally comes the need to deal appropriately (being assertive, expressing what is true for you, making amends, and so on) with the present *as present* and with the past *as past* (for example, talking to a good friend, getting a good therapist).

Riding the Waves

1. Recognize that you are *in a storm* (Step One).

2. Make sure you're breathing into your stomach and are exhaling slowly.

3. Anchor yourself in the present moment (where am I, what's going on around me, what can I see, hear, smell, touch) and forget trying to do anything. Wait until it passes (Step Two)

4. Decide what *really* has to do with the present (Step Three).

5. Deal with it realistically *as the present* (Step Four).

6. Decide what has to do with the past (Step Three – messages from unfinished business, overlaid onto the present)

7. Recognize the source and do some housecleaning (Step Four).

This skill of riding the waves of an emotional storm involves a great deal of awareness, as well as the integrity to take responsibility for your own emotional response, rather than blaming it on someone else. In the long run, you and you alone are responsible for creating your own peace and your own happiness. As we shall see later, this becomes a crucial skill in the creation of vital and lasting relationships.

*****

There is another phenomenon that is more like being stranded in a desert rather than being swamped by a flood of emotions. This occurs when we are faced with moments of not knowing what to do or where to go in our lives, moments of massive confusion and indecision, moments in which we feel profoundly empty, without purpose or passion. In these moments, all kinds of feelings arise. Some of these are helpful; some are false alarms. Many of them tell us that it is not okay, even dangerous, to be in a desert, in a place that feels confusing or empty, with no signposts. It is a time of potential and profound transition.

In the Old Testament, we read of the passage of the Jewish people out of Egypt into the Promised Land. It wasn't easy. They had to cross the Red Sea, then spend forty years wandering through the desert before reaching their destination. No compass, no travel centers, no ATMs, and no GPS. How do you say "bummer" in Yiddish?

There must have been many times when they doubted their decision to escape from bondage and wished for their predictable existence under Egyptian rule. Confusion and doubt were most likely rampant. Guidance, however, came from Moses, and by trusting in his word, his patience, and his relationship with God, they eventually made it through the desert.

We often have desert experiences of our own. Often without knowing it, we are in the middle of a powerful time of transition, a calling to a new way of being and living. In times such as these, our job, relationships, the ways in which we spend our time no longer have the same meaning, no longer satisfy us. We feel confused, empty, bored, anxious, or all of the above. These emotions can be very difficult to tolerate, particularly if we're not listening to the messages they bring. Given this difficulty, it is not unusual to begin to wish for the old ways of living and being, even if it means a return to a life devoid of meaning or passion, a life often replete with addiction, control, approval, life-draining jobs, or dying relationships.

Confusion, emptiness, and boredom can be signals from our own internal Moses, our emotional guidance system, letting us know that it is time to take the risk of leaving home and entering the desert. It is time to cross into a new and larger way of living

Anna wanted to break it off with Vince, her boyfriend of several years. As attractive and bright as she was, she had always doubted her worth, so she hooked up with a good-looking and ambitious young man. Without knowing it, however, a good part of her was in the relationship as a way of getting approval and affirmation. It was, to some degree, a deficit-based relationship. "Make me feel worthy, wanted, and accepted," some young part of her was saying, "and I'll orbit around you, a moon to your sun."

Unknowingly, she spent much of the time over those three years trying to predict his needs and moods, until one night, after getting drunk, he exploded at her. He wanted sex, but she wasn't interested in being anywhere near him.

"Get into bed, you bitch!" he screamed. "I work all the time, so is it asking too fucking much!?"

"No way," she replied. "Not when you're like this."

"Then get the hell out of here! Get out!"

And so she did. She had discovered a dark side of her boyfriend that she couldn't live with. The degree to which she had been living her life and her worth through him became crystal clear in that moment. Now she was in the desert, not knowing what to do.

"I feel like my head is going to explode open," she said in a phone call to me late one evening. "Vince keeps on calling, telling me that I'm throwing these past years away. He says he'll change, that's he's learned his lesson, and will do anything to keep me. And he wants to know now if I want to give the relationship another try or not. How am I supposed to know?"

Anna couldn't know much for sure. Without realizing it, she had slowly been growing a healthy sense of herself, no longer needed Vince's approval as much, and had fallen out of love with him. That one night had brought her change of heart into relief, but still she was confused, and Vince wanted an answer.

"He'll have to wait," I told her. "His needs and his comfort are not your responsibility. You need time and space to listen to yourself: what is it that will make *you* feel good, and will bring *you* happiness? How do you feel about *you* when you're with him and when you're *not* with him?"

Her desert experience had begun. It was time to let strong feelings of fear (of being without him), guilt (for leaving him), and anxiety (what will happen to my life) come and go. It was time to listen to her Self.

When we are in such times of transition, a great deal of anxiety is generated by the belief that we *should* know what to do, where to go, how to feel, rather than allowing the confusion. As the German poet, Rainer Maria Rilke, has described in his *Letters to a Young Poet*, some questions cannot be answered at will from an armchair. These are the larger questions about roads not traveled, relationships to be pursued or discontinued, risks to be taken or not.

> Have patience with everything that remains unsolved in your heart. Try to love the questions themselves, like locked rooms and like books written in a foreign language. Do not now look for the answers. They cannot now be given to you because you could not live them. It is a question of experiencing everything. At present you need to live the question. Perhaps you will gradually, without even noticing it, find yourself experiencing the answer, some distant day.

Such questions at the crossroads of life junctures can leave us in a place of not knowing. It is here, as with the storm, that we must hold on, let feelings come and go, recognize/check their messages, and listen.

We begin by recognizing the erroneous messages of "shoulds" and "shouldn'ts" that tell us we must know and be in control at all times, even when that's not possible. We must check the reality of the fears that orbit around potential change. When this is done and anxiety begins to subside, we can listen to the reverberations from those wells of wisdom that exist within each of us.

Anger, frustration, fear of being lost or left behind, fear of being wrong, and fear of what others may think or fear of hurting others assault us in our desert experience.

Boredom, the feeling that tells us that we *may* be without the stimulus we need to feel alive, can also mislead us at such times, if we hold onto the belief that we must be *doing* something or having some experience in order to feel satisfied and worthwhile. As with anxiety, however, if we watch and let boredom pass in moments of not knowing, we may stumble into a silence that speaks loudly to our deepest desires.

Surviving the Desert

1. **Allow the confusion, rather than insisting on knowing what to do.**

2. **Be aware of the feelings (anxiety, shame, anger, sadness) and reality check their messages, particularly the ones that tell us that we "should" know or "should" have answers and solutions.**

3. **Pay special attention to any fear and check the message attached to it.**

4. **When the warning emotions settle down, begin to listen to what feels positive and good. Remember that emotions indicate what is right for us, not just what is wrong or potentially dangerous.**

The desert can be a place of infinite possibility, not unlike the emptiness Buddhism speaks of. In Western terminology, it is the death/resurrection bridge between a way of life that has left us knowing that there has to be more, and a way of living vibrantly from the inside out. It is a fertile void, if we can weather the emotional onslaughts, recognize them and the fear-based messages that drive them, so that finally, as Rilke suggests, we might awaken one morning and discover that we have lived our way into the answers we sought.

Chapter 10:

Empty Bowl, Full Bowl

"Thanks to emptiness, everything is possible."

Nagarjuna (2nd Century)

The calm that follows a storm or a transitional desert experience can also frighten us, because we are no longer consumed by our busyness or our fears, no longer caught up in the identities that our negative stories create (I'm bad, dirty, unworthy, inadequate, unlovable). It can be difficult to recognize ourselves without the old masks and roles.

As damaging as these limiting and false identities can be, we are used to them, and their absence can leave us feeling lost and naked. If I'm not working and productive, who am I? If I am not getting the praise, the rewards, the sex, the pleasure I seek, what am I worth? If I'm not perfect, who will like me?

In the calm after an emotional storm, the peace we feel is the result of having been cleansed, at least for the time being, of false identities and the need for someone else's approval. We're in a place of no-thing, yet poised at the edge of everything we've yearned for. It's almost as if we don't recognize the stripped-down version of our self. The path through this place demands that we face and feel the emotions that we fear might kill us

Kim is slumped in front of me, feet tucked under her India-print skirt, cross-legged on the couch of my office. In her mid-twenties, with blonde hair and a Nordic face, she can light up a room with her presence. Now she looks up and says, "I have to be honest. Jimmy called me up the other day, drunk, and I still invited him over, and we had sex. And then he just blows me off. He doesn't call, just disappears on me! So I really was upset. I wasn't going to drink, but I binged, just to fill up that awful hole. But then I started getting into my 'fat' thinking and couldn't stand the food in my stomach. I just threw it up."

Kim came to my office, referred by a clinic for eating disorders, by way of a rural, Pennsylvania town that once bustled with a coal industry that left the community after it had taken what it needed. Large homes line the main street into this town, formerly castles of the industry's management. They've long since been bought up by judges, funeral homes, and real estate brokers.

Those still living there work as contractors, retailers, and in blue-collar jobs. People here don't talk about personal things very much. They just keep putting one foot in front of the other, making it to the weekend.

This is where Kim's history begins, a history that bleeds through as she makes her way through nursing school while struggling with relationships. This is where the abuse took place, the heavy drinking and drugging, the empty sex, all before she was fourteen. It was here that her mother's anxiety taught Kim that she was never good enough; here that her father's absence and emotional distance became his way of dealing with not knowing what the hell to do with this kid.

She was twelve the night she blurted out the story of her sexual abuse by an older teen, spewed it out with the vomit that reeked of beer and Seagram's. The families gathered one evening to deal with the event. The parents of the older boy were there, her mother was there, her father was busy at work. No one really said anything. No one ever asked her how she was doing.

Years later, in the lobby of a local bank, she bumped into this boy and still felt the shame color her light complexion, still felt she would never be good enough.

"Tell me more, Kim," I ask, "about the binge and purge."

"Oh, god, it sucked! It sucked so bad! I felt so damned lonely. And then empty. And I just didn't know how to deal with that. I tried everything and finally had to get away just to talk to someone so I didn't have to feel that empty thing."

"Kim, this might be big, very big. Would you be willing to go back there?"

"You mean that feeling?"

"Yeah."

"Well, okay, but I'm not really thrilled about this."

"When was the worst moment?" I ask.

"Just after I got rid of the food."

"Remember, you always have your breath to come back to, this office to come back to. So for now, bring yourself to that moment, that worst moment, and notice whatever you notice."

"It's so, so empty. Like I can't stand it. It aches, and it's dark. I just hate this. I want to fill it with something, or someone. And it's scary. Now my breathing is getting short and fast."

The storm is building. When it hits what feels like a small and insignificant boat in the middle of a turbulent vastness, one can only hold onto the mast for life.

"God, it's so dark. Scares the shit out of me. How do people stand this? And I've been here, you know, this feeling, and I'm so tired of it! I had this as a kid, and when I was in my teens, and now, still, I'm twenty-five, and it's still here!"

"Hold onto the breath, then touch the dark, then breathe, then touch the dark," I repeat, like a mantra to keep her afloat.

"And it aches in there, and now it's sad, so sad. I don't think this sadness will ever let up." Tears flow, cleansing waters.

"You're not alone, Kim. Breathe. Breathe and just let it all be."

"Now I'm just pissed, pissed at everyone. And just pissed that I get so damned needy! "

"Watch the 'needy'," I suggest. "See what happens next."

"Now it's just sad again, that old sad, sad feeling..."

The silence seems as long as her adolescent years.

"It's getting quiet now," she finally states. "Real still. Like nothing's there, but it's different from before. It's very, very still."

"And how is that?"

"Well, okay," she pauses. "Just weird."

Eventually, Kim lifts her head, color dawning across her face. The storm has passed. She has made a heroine's journey from a place of sterile emptiness, through the emotions and false self-beliefs that have imprisoned her since childhood, and now into a place of fertile possibilities.

"Where are you now, Kim, with all of this?"

"It's just weird!" she says. "Like Jimmy just doesn't matter right now, and I, I…." She pauses, then continues. "It's not even about him. I'm just, just different. I don't feel so needy, so damned desperate."

With the courage of awareness, Kim stepped into the cleansing waters. All that was unessential about her could leave, as it were, on its own. The urges, the distractions, the identities all departed, jobless in the new order of things. At least for that moment, but now is all we ever have.

I say, "It could be that even with no one there, in some way, you've never really been alone."

I recall the words of Steven Levine, quoting an Indian guru: "The mind creates the abyss; the heart must cross it." The storytelling part of Kim's mind had convinced her that she was bad, dirty, never good enough. Her heart needed the courage to move through those false perceptions and the painful emotions attached to them into a place of no-story, where the freedom of true Self-hood begins.

In Japan, when one family visits another, there is a custom of gift-giving. One of these gifts is an empty bowl. The emptiness represents not poverty, but infinite possibilities. This is the gift the visitors bring. And in Kim's work, this is the place her heart revealed.

*****

Mich comes in to see me the day after my meeting with Kim. He is not Nordic, not average, not your run-of-the-mill kid. He is a seventeen-year-old boy with Downs syndrome, who likes to pick at his feet and the pimple on his arm, loves to play his harmonica while listening to the soundtrack of "Chicago" on his Walkman headphones.

With his mother trailing slowly behind, he charges up the stairs to the office, announcing his arrival with a burst of enthusiasm. And with a pumpkin to show me. Fall has arrived as well.

He drops an overweight body into his favorite recliner, dumps his knapsack on the floor, and simply beams. Mom, a bit out of breath, makes it to the couch, and we begin the ritual of checking in with each other.

Mich is learning to notice others. After years of being attended to as the "special child," it's time for him to learn to step out of his self-absorption and expand his awareness to include the needs and feelings of others. I've told him how good it feels when he asks me how I'm doing.

"So, how are *you*?" he asks me.

"Pretty good," I reply, being as honest as I can about my mid-afternoon, nap-fantasizing energy slump. "And how are *you* doing?"

"Peachy!" he bubbles.

"Zero to ten?" I ask, using our scale for all seasons.

"Hmmm, I'd say eight!"

"Great. And how do you think mom's doing?"

"I don't know," he answers, in a tone that says it's not his problem.

"Well, take a look at mom. What do you notice?"

"She looks tired. Maybe a six?"

Turning to his mother, I ask, "How close is that, mom?"

"Pretty good. I'd say that at this very moment, with all the rushing around, that that's real close."

"Hey, good noticing, Mich!" I offer.

We begin our brief review of the week before Michael and I have our time to ourselves. His mother once told me through tears, that our time belongs to Mich--it is the one place in his life where he is not being scheduled, structured and directed towards someone else's goal for him.

Mich doesn't have much to say about the week. He has that pulled-back look all of a sudden that tells me that something has happened.

His mother encourages him. "Mich, tell Andrew what happened yesterday."

"I don't want to talk about that," comes the reply with a pout.

"Is it okay if I tell him? Because that's why we're here."

"Okay," he mutters.

His mother proceeds to relate incidents the day before, when Mich was disrespectful not only to three teachers--teachers, his mother reminds me, he has known and loved "forever." Mich pulls further into his silent pout.

We begin to explore. I draw circles and describe what other people have taught me about "acting out behaviors." I tell him that there is always a reason, always a payoff. I hold the back of my hand towards him, stretch out my fingers, each one representing a choice, a reason people do disrespectful things to others.

"Mich," I begin, realizing that with the visual aid of my hand, I have his attention, "when people do things like talking back, they sometimes are feeling hurt, angry, sad and left out, or that 'something's-wrong-with-me' feeling. Were any of those feelings going on for you yesterday?"

He leans forward and pushes the last two fingers together.

"Those two."

And then comes the story. His best friend, Jimmy, another teenager with Downs syndrome, went to Florida with his family and hadn't taken Mich with them.

"He's like my other brother. And his family is my other family. I had to stay here and work and take care of things while they were away. I hate that! I should be with them."

"Were you angry at all? " I venture.

"Yeah, that, too."

The story becomes clear to all of us, and after his mother leaves, I ask Mich if he wants to clear out those feelings.

"I want to talk about something else."

"Well, we've done this before, you know, like cleaning out a cut so that it can get better and not bother you anymore. It might sting a bit, but it goes away pretty quickly."

"Just a little," he concedes, "but then I want to talk about something else."

"Sure," I agree.

I'm intending, at this point, to loosen up the blocked responses, forgetting that there is a phoenix waiting to rise. Mich is about to remind me.

I begin to move my hand horizontally back and forth in front of his eyes, asking him to track my bilateral motions, while focusing on the feelings connected to being left behind. Mich is used to this method for neutralizing the effects of trauma and simply painful events. We've done this before with success, and we have a positive track record.

After the first set of eye movements, I ask him to breathe and let me know how strong the feelings are. To give us both a baseline, I spread my hands outward to indicate strong feelings. Pulling my hands to about three feet apart, I remind him:

"This is for somewhere in the middle, and when I put my hands together, that's just about all gone or completely gone. Okay?"

"Yeah," he mutters. At this point he's not the happiest of campers.

"So where are the feelings at?" I ask.

"A little better," he states, a bit more energy in his voice.

"Show me," I say, and he spreads his hands halfway between midpoint and extreme.

"Let's try it again."

I move my fingers back and forth again for a couple of minutes, stop and ask the same question, "So what's happening with the feelings now?"

He brings his hands together and tells me he is feeling much better. We do one more set of eye movements,

I stop, and before I can ask, he reaches over to me, his familiar smile reappearing, pushes my hands completely together and says, "I love Jimmy!"

It was there all along--this deep connection with a disabled brother, bigger than jealousy, deeper than any perceived abandonment. Mich simply needed support in composting initial reactions so that the best in him could grow, so he could be that which he most truly is.

I sit there, surprised, even though I have had such moments before. "Let's do that once more, Mitch, to make sure those old feelings are gone."

"Okay," he bubbles. One more set, and I hear, "I love Jimmy!" again.

*****

The breakthrough moments experienced by Kim and Mich have a universal quality to them, moments when we remember that miraculous place, the empty bowl filled with all possibilities, that pulsates at the very core of our true being. We all exist on the continuum between a life fully lived or not, between the familiar comfort zones and the unknown territory of growth. In these sessions, the journey was not really about the presence or absence of a disability, or even problems. Kim and Mich simply and yet profoundly touched the heart of who they most truly are.

There's always something to learn and understanding that can be deepened. One of my early teachers was the game of basketball. On the asphalt courts of Brooklyn, I learned that there's always a new move to master, and if you don't get it, someone will "take you to school" and teach you on the courts the hard way. As a point guard, or ball mover as it was called in those days, I spent hours, summer and winter, on the outdoor courts, learning to control the dribble and to protect the ball as I worked to deliver it to my teammates. Over and over, I would work both hands, so that my body would remember. One moment of forgetfulness and the ball could be stolen, an easy lay up for the other team, and a game could be lost.

During these few days at the office, it felt as if I had been taken to school once again. I was reminded of something I've always believed, but which, at times, sounded only faintly from a distance: I don't give my clients anything they don't already have. That which heals, the saving grace, so to speak, can never be damaged in each of us; it is always poised and ready to spring into new life.

The tagline on our office letterhead used to read, "We carry within us the wonders we seek." Kim and Mich helped me remember that.

Chapter 11:

What Color is Your Lens?

Simon just didn't get it. When he lived in his shell, things were predictable. Critters were simply critters. He did what his mother advised. There was a time and a place for everything.

Now, on his own, the world seemed so much more confusing. Not only were there days when the swamp seemed to hold one surprise after another, but creatures and things didn't seem to stay the same. The bullfrog was one such animal.

On some evenings, the deep voices of the bullfrogs sounded like music, resonant and rhythmic. At other times, those same voices were unbelievably irritating, causing Simon to wish he could just pull his old shell back over his head.

Evening itself could be soothing at times, frightening at others. The sun was warm and inviting in one moment, but without his shell, Simon also found the day's heat burning, even threatening. The same creatures, the same events were really never the same.

Most interesting were his reactions to those closest to him: his mother and his dear friend, Ronald. Oh, how he appreciated his mom sometimes, because she always did her best to be there for him. At other times, however, she seemed more like the wicked witch of the swamp or a jail keeper. It was somewhat the same with Ronald. He could seem to be the best friend a turtle could have. He could also seem to Simon to be just an irritating mouse with attitude.

"Appearances change," Simon thought. "Why is that? Why don't things stay the same?"

"Because you don't stay the same," came the edgy voice of the mind-reading mouse. Whenever Simon ran into these dilemmas, Ronald had the annoying habit of popping up almost out of nowhere, inevitably with the right answer.

"Now that makes no sense," replied Simon with some irritation. "Things are supposed to be the way they are!"

"And who says so?" asked Ronald. "Think of it this way. If you have an upset stomach, like the time you ate that weird bug, how did things look to you for most of that day?"

"Awful," recalled Simon. "If I had to color that day, I would color it green and grey."

"Exactly!" replied Ronald, puffing up. "And if you have a headache, is your mom more annoying? If you're feeling confused and irritated, do I get on your nerves?"

"Yep, on both counts," answered Simon.

"So, with both things and people, we don't really see them as they are, do we? We see them as we are. Get it?"

"Oh, oh, my," stammered Simon, as a light seemed to go on somewhere in the middle of his brain.

*****

"Objects in your rearview mirror are closer than they appear," advises the message on the passenger-side mirror of most vehicles. Life would be easier if relationships came with similar warnings: "The person you are about to marry is more insensitive than he appears;" "Your boss is not as critical as she appears;" "Your best friend is not as angry at you as she appears;" "Life is not as unsafe as it appears;" "Your legs are not as heavy as they seem."

Whether it is a relationship with another, ourselves, or with life in general, we rarely experience it as he/she/it is. We always look through the lens of our internal state, our beliefs, feelings, physical condition, and past experiences. This lens experiencing, as I term it, is a low-grade form of projection that goes on most of the time. Projection is an as-needed form of defense; lens experiencing is what we do most of the time.

I spill a cup of coffee on my lap over breakfast and think, "This is going be one of those days, I can tell!" And so it turns out. I have a headache that just won't quit, and for some reason, everything annoys the hell out of me. Present events, as well as physical conditions, can affect how we experience things. It gets even worse when our past becomes involved in coloring how we see the present.

If I grew up with a critical parent, I might find there's no such thing as constructive criticism, at least as far as I'm concerned. If I had been sexually abused, I might cringe at the thought of anyone touching me. If I watched my mother struggle to make ends meet growing up, I might never earn enough to feel secure. If I recall the images of the Twin Towers on television, I might view every Near Easterner as dangerous.

We are always experiencing life through a lens. It is just part of being human. The problem occurs when we are not aware that a lens is even there, leaving us convinced that what we experience is the way it actually is. And there's the rub.

I was teaching a college course, and Lynette, who usually needed to challenge me in order to let others know what she knew, was falling asleep in front of me. As a matter of fact, she was snoring. My storytelling lens kicked in.

"I'm working my tail off, keeping the group engaged, and she's just nodding off! Really pisses me off! Won't let herself be taught and now she just has to blow me off totally."

So I thought.

I found out the following day that Lynette was struggling with a sleep disorder, hadn't slept for days, was medicated, and in a zombie state half the time. I had allowed my history with her to completely color the present moment.

Have you ever noticed a "weird" or "annoyed" or "totally disinterested" look on someone's face, and been convinced that they were reacting to you? Then you react as if your assumption, your interpretation were true? Then, your negative reaction to them really gets them going, so they, in fact, do react negatively to you, proving the "truth" of your perceptions. You've created the reactions that you imagined in the first place. Later you find out that the person was dealing with a head cold or was just having a bad hair day that had nothing to do with you.

Our perceptions typically activate a feeling. Rather than act as if our assumptions triggering the emotion are objective reality, we need to apply Step Three. It is time to check out the message with the feeling.

Janice was admittedly a control freak. She knew this and everyone around her knew this, particularly her husband

and two children. She and they simply assumed that this was the way it had to be.

Her husband, Nate, had his own dark side. He never felt good enough, so he always worked hard at his job to prove to others that he was not as inadequate as he believed deep down inside. This often resulted in his working late, something Janice found very disturbing.

"He's probably having an affair, or staying late to talk to a 'just friend' kind of woman," she thought over and over, until she was convinced of her suspicions. She kept these thoughts to herself, becoming distant and resentful towards Nate in the process.

A few times she confronted Nate with these suspicions, and every time he vehemently denied it. But by that time, her assumptions had become so strong that nothing Nate said convinced her otherwise. This persisted until Nate began to come home later and later just to stay away from her accusations and cold resentment. Needless to say, in time he found someone at the office who would listen to him. Janice's worst fear had become a reality, one to which she had unknowingly contributed.

If Janice had been willing to check out her assumptions earlier, it might have been easier for her to hear what was driving Nate's need to work so hard. If she had been able to express her emotional truth ("I'm so afraid, I'm so hurt when I think that....") in a non-blaming way, Nate might have been able to understand the impact of his overworking on his marriage. He might even have begun to explore what drove him into a behavior that was creating a wedge between him and his wife.

Instead, each went to his/her private world, interpreted the other's behaviors in the worst light, and reacted as if the interpretations were absolute truth.

"He's having an affair for sure."

"She's got to make everyone miserable, just out of some sadistic need to control!"

Janice's underlying feeling state was fear and anxiety. In general and, particularly, with Nate, she was always convinced that something terrible was about to happen. She was controlled by catastrophic expectations. Hence, her need to control the world around her in order to keep that anxiety inside under control.

Nate responded to her accusations first with anger, then with the hurt and the shame of never being enough. He interpreted her behavior as coming from an innate need to control and keep others in a one-down position.

In not checking the messages out and not attending to the layers of emotions, they each missed a lot. Janice was unaware of how much her anxiety ruled her behavior and how much insecurity drove Nate's work habits. Nate hadn't a clue about the insecurity behind his late hours at the job, and he had no idea of the fears and anxiety that motivated most of Janice's suspicions and controlling behavior.

They didn't "get" each other; they certainly didn't "get" themselves.

A variation on the theme of assumptions resulting from our lens occurs when we accurately perceive an annoying characteristic in another, but our negative experience of that characteristic in the past amplifies what we experience in the present.

Vern was a medical pathologist. He examined biopsies and bodies to diagnose and to determine cause of death. He was a self-proclaimed "anal kind of guy," and his reports were incredibly thorough and time-consuming. His perfectionism had saved his emotional life as a teenager, when he found himself sharply criticized by his mother and her new boyfriend. At times, his perfectionistic style impressed and intimidated younger colleagues. At times it made them a bit crazy.

Enter Justine, a younger female colleague with a feminist chip on her shoulder. She was aggressive, competitive, and driven to succeed and to prove her worth and competence. Her history is no surprise: she had been raised by a father with an obsessive-compulsive personality in whose eyes his daughter was never perfect enough.

Justine's take on Vern was that he was an arrogant bastard, especially when he tilted his head back and to the side, obviously criticizing her or her work. Vern's take on Justine was that she was a castrating bitch, who had to be on top, so to speak, needing to monitor his every move and report it to their director. Each was convinced of the accuracy of their perception. Neither of them checked it out. They dared not. This was war, and professional survival was the name of the game.

The time, energy, and productivity lost as a result of this battle were immeasurable. If Vern had known that Justine's aggressiveness covered years of damage at the hands of a patriarchal childhood, where dad's word was law and mom curled into a ball of retreat at any sign of her husband's displeasure, she might not have seemed so threatening. If Justine knew how disdainful Vern's mother had been towards him, the surviving child after a younger sister had died in a house fire, she might have seen his "attitude" as more protective than critical.

Unfortunately, no one in their facility was aware and skilled enough to sit them both down to focus on understanding, rather than being right and safe. If they had *become known to each other*, they might have been able to soften and listen rather than defend and attack. They might have learned that, although each actually embodied some of the characteristics the other hated, the distortion and intensity of their perceptions was due to the past. Learning the truth of each other at this deeper level might have made for better relationships and much better business.

This is the Velcro effect in action. For whatever you dislike from your past to project onto and stick to the other, some of that quality has to exist in your target. The *intensity* of what you perceive, however, most likely belongs to you and your history.

What children assume about parents and what parents assume about their children is another arena where lens distortion often leads to painful misunderstandings, particularly in the adolescent-parent relationship. The adolescent lens is colored not only by developmental needs (independence, autonomy), but by biochemistry as well. Raging hormones add a distinct color to the adolescent perceptual lens. Meanwhile, parents, already stressed with the demands of work, creating a household, parenting other children, marriage and finances, are often time bombs ready to explode. Much of what they see in their teenage child is disrespect, ingratitude and selfishness. "Go to your room until you're thirty!" is their frequent fantasy.

It is a very difficult task that is mostly up to the parents, being the responsible ones, the ones who model stepping out of the unchecked assumptions and moving into a place of understanding, rather than having to be right. It is up to the parents to take the lead in checking assumptions and telling the truth, because they invited their children into the world.

Sherry's daughter, Alexis, wanted more freedom, but Sherry was not about to loosen the reins, even though Alexis was seventeen. The tighter Sherry tried to control what she couldn't do--which kids Alexis would speak to at school, which boys she danced with at the prom--the more rebellious her daughter became. Alexis began to sneak out at night after Sherry was asleep, and the stench of cigarette smoke and alcohol began to infiltrate her clothing. Sherry was in a state of panic.

They both appeared in my office, Sherry's face showing lines of worry and lack of sleep. Alexis just sat and scowled.

"She's crazy!" Alexis lit into her mother. "She's locking me up, chaining me in my own bedroom!"

I allow a few moments for the adolescent drama to pass.

"And when she does things like that, what's it like for you?"

"I become a crazy person! I just want to break things. I want to piss her off. I want OUT!"

"And when you want to do those things, what's happening inside?"

"I don't know….I guess I feel trapped, like I can't breathe. Like she *so* doesn't get me!"

"But." Sherry injects, "I only want to keep you safe!"

"From what," retorts Alexis, "the world, *life*?! You don't want me to *breathe!*"

"I don't want things to happen to you, that's all…"

Sherry pauses, weighing her words. "When I was your age, my parents didn't really give a shit about what I was doing. They were too busy fighting, drinking, then fighting more. One time, one of many times, I snuck out at night and met this guy I had a thing for. I got pregnant. He was much older, but he didn't give a shit either. So I had the abortion by myself. I just couldn't tell my parents."

Tears slipped down her face, seeming to erase the worried lines, painting a different emotional picture.

"I'm just terrified that something like that is going to happen to you."

I look over at Alexis. The anger has left her face. Her eyes are moist.

"Why didn't you tell me, Mom?"

They're now holding onto each other, walls of misunderstanding gone.

"Ashamed, I guess."

At this moment of truth, Alexis *sees* Sherry differently, mostly because Sherry took the risk to be real, to let herself *be seen.*

There was very little for me to do or say, other than to ask: "Alexis, your mom has, hopefully, made things clearer to

139

you. Not that she should continue to overly control you, but by letting you know what she's afraid of. Is there anything else that you want your mom to understand about you?"

A few tissues later, Alexis answers, "It's just that, well, I know that there have to be rules and stuff, but sometimes it feels like I'm *dying*...like I can't breathe, and then I just want to do *any*thing to break loose, even stupid stuff."

Our time together soon came to an end, and they left seeing each other through a new lens. Sherry's own history was coloring her view of her daughter's behaviors, and Alexis' developmental need to be on her own could only allow her to see her mother as the oppressive enemy. Vulnerability eventually made it unnecessary for them to defend or attack. They were becoming known to each other.

Steps in Checking Out Your Lens

1. **BE AWARE of the lens through which you experience everything.**

2. **REMEMBER that the lens can be created by your own history (projection), by previous experience with a person (pigeon holing), or by your mental, physical and/or emotional state.**

3. **TAKE RESPONSIBILITY for your own internal experience.**

4. **HAVE THE COURAGE to check out your perceptions and assumptions.**

PART FOUR

Living a Life of Emotional Honesty

Chapter 12:

The A.R.T. of Emotional Honesty

Ronald noticed that Simon was growing a bit distant from everyone. He was back in his moping mode. He was still painting the swamp critters, but he didn't seem to connect with them as much. The bullfrogs, the beavers, and the masked raccoon wondered if they had done something to offend Simon, since he was so silent. Even the fox, who didn't have much to do with anyone, noticed the change.

Ronald sighed and pulled himself up, realizing it was time to do something about it. He made his way through the grass and the reeds at the water's edge, until he was standing next to Simon.

"What's up, big guy?" he began.

"Nothing."

"I don't believe you," said Ronald flatly. "You're moping again."

"So?" Simon put down his brushes and slumped onto the edge of a log.

"So, something's going on, and you're not talking. You don't look all that happy. As a matter of fact, you look ticked off!"

"Well, maybe I am," said Simon. "Maybe I'm tired of those beavers slapping their tails in the water all the time. Maybe I'm ticked off at that bullfrog's weird voice. Maybe I don't know if the raccoon is going to steal one of my brushes or not. And I hate the way that fox stares all the time.

"You know, they don't realize how hard it is to concentrate out here. It's as if I'm invisible, or that what I'm doing isn't important to them. Don't they get it?"

"Probably not," said Ronald. "How are they supposed to know?"

*****

The first two steps in emotional competence (being aware of and having the feeling) can suffice in situations in which we only have to deal with ourselves and our own thoughts and feelings. When it comes to relationships, however, it is usually necessary to step outside our private world and enter the realm of dialogue. Typical requests from couples upon their first visit to my office sound something like, "We want to save our marriage. We want to communicate better!" They are usually seeking methods and recipes for making things better.

After I diplomatically ask them if they want to save *that* marriage or create something better, I let them know that there is a process that needs to be in place before communication skills can be effective.

Many self-help systems explain these basic skills. They are mostly ineffective without awareness of what's happening internally, responsibility for one's internal experiences, and the courage to tell the emotional truth about it. You might know how to say something, but if you don't know what's really going on inside, or if you're not willing to express it, you have the form without the substance. Only an empty shell.

The equation for good communication that has evolved from my experiences with couples is: **A + R + T= Vital Relationship**. Awareness plus responsibility plus telling the truth will give you the relationship you've always wanted to come home to.

Awareness, always our first step, lets us know what is really going on inside. Awareness puts us in touch with our thoughts, our emotional signals, and our contentment or lack thereof.

Cynthia had been carrying on an affair for five-and-a-half years when she came to see me. She had finally been found out, and felt her life coming apart. She was highly respected in her community, had raised three children, who were now out and on their own, living successful lives. She was currently the head of a Human Resource department for a Fortune 500 company. Her husband, Roger, an engineering project manager for the same company, was, according to Cynthia, a great provider and good father when he wasn't working.

"I don't know how I could do this, day after day, year after year," she told me. "I mean, I really do have a strong sense of right and wrong, except for this."

A bright, ethical, and kind woman cheated on her husband for over half a decade. How could this be?

As we spoke, it became clear that Cynthia had been starving emotionally. She had married wanting to be taken care of, but no longer needed such rescuing. Instead, she craved emotional connection, something Roger failed at on a daily basis. When she began the affair, she had already spent close to twenty years denying herself an awareness of her emotional needs. As she fell into an emotional affair with a work colleague, she pushed more and more out of her awareness.

Cynthia ignored how empty and bored she felt with her husband. She pushed aside any guilt that would have indicated that she was far outside her integrity with her colleague, now her affair partner, despite the upstanding way in which she lived the rest of her life. She also ignored the fear that arose whenever she thought of facing the truth of her marriage. Cynthia had managed her deceit by blocking from her awareness not only emotional responses to her present situation, but also her fear of conflict that was rooted in experiences with her father. For five-and-a-half years her guidance system, which bore messages from her past as well as her present, was kept out of her awareness until Roger noticed a repeated unlisted phone number on their monthly Verizon bill.

And so it came to pass that Roger finally confronted his wife, who could not deny the obvious anymore. Lack of integrity demands an enormous amount of energy, since it is a path that goes against the grain of authentic living. Now Cynthia sat in front of me, exhausted, experiencing many of the feelings that had been blocked from her awareness for years. Awareness, though, is only the first part of our equation.

Even when we are aware of our inner experience, i.e., our feelings, thoughts, beliefs, assumptions, memories, images, we still must take responsibility for them. They are the result of our own internal system of choice, perception, interpretation and, often, projection. As long as we blame our thoughts and feelings, our frustration, boredom, or misery on someone or something else, we are operating from a victim position and are unable to respond (response-ability) effectively to a situation. We give the power over our well-being to someone else.

Cynthia began the race for the victim position.

"He just wasn't there, for years, I mean. I didn't even realize it, but I couldn't take it anymore. I needed someone who saw me as more than a baby maker and housekeeper."

"What kept you from bringing this up to him?" I asked.

"Well, you just can't talk to him, you know? He's either tired, irritable, or distant."

"And what kept you from bringing that up to him?"

"You just don't get it!" she fired back. "That's just not possible with him!"

"And you stayed with all of that because…?"

"I feel like you're making all this out to be my fault!"

With that statement, it became clear that Cynthia was more invested in being right than in being connected with herself; more in need of avoiding what her emotions were telling her than taking responsibility for her life. Her emotions seemed to be saying: (1) I'm not happy with this marriage as it exists, and haven't been happy for a long time; (2) the way I've handled this is not in my integrity; and (3) it's time to take responsibility for my own happiness and make choices that will support the life I want. Cynthia needed to embrace and take full responsibility for her microscopic truth, her internal reality.

"Microscopic truthfulness" is a term first used, as far as I am aware, by Brenda Ueland in her book *If You Want to Write.* She speaks of the necessary integrity of the writer:

> Gradually, by writing, you will learn more and more to be free, to say all you think; and at the same time you will learn never to lie to yourself, never to pretend and attitudinize. But only by writing and by long, patient, serious work will you find your true self.
>
> And why find it? Because it is, I think, your immortal soul and the life of the Spirit, and if we can only free it and respect it and not run it down, and let it move and work, it is the way to be happier and greater.

Gay and Kathlyn Hendricks wrote about the "unarguable truth" in *Conscious Loving*. Our unarguable truth refers to our internal truth, the way things are inside, even though it may not line up with external reality or with someone else's truth. It is how things are for us, and it must be our starting point in any dialogue. It must be spoken of in the first person if we are to own it. By claiming our feelings, thoughts, and assumptions, and expressing them responsibly, it becomes easier for our partner to take in what we are expressing, rather than defend and attack back.

"Unarguable" does not mean that what we experience must be the truth for everyone. It is our personal truth in a given moment, subject to change in the course of any communication or discussion. Until we learn to give voice to our own truth, there can be no true relating, because we haven't shown up for the encounter. The unarguable truth demands expression in relationships if they are to remain healthy and vital.

Cynthia had many reasons for being unhappy, but she was still using her childhood strategies of avoidance and deception. As a grown woman, those strategies were backfiring.

In our sessions, she gained a sense of responsibility for her own life, both inner and outer. Guilt, anger, and sadness, though, still bothered her. She had yet to sit down with Roger to tell him her unarguable truth.

They agreed to come in together for the purpose of expressing their "state of the union." The intent of the session wasn't to save or end a marriage, but to have Cynthia and Roger become more known to each other. After years of unhappiness and lack of truth-telling, Cynthia finally mustered the courage to be microscopically authentic with her husband.

"I've been miserable for a long time," she began, "and I'm not blaming you for it."

The journey of a thousand miles had begun. Eventually, they decided to part ways, but now as better people and better friends. Both became "happier and greater," as Brenda Ueland described it, for telling and hearing the unarguable truth.

The A.R.T. of Vital Relationship

Be AWARE of your internal experience

Take RESPONSIBILITY for your internal experience

Tell the unarguable TRUTH of your internal experience

Once the A.R.T. equation is in place, skills in verbalizing the truth are needed. They rely primarily on expressing *your* truth, rather than telling the other person what their truth is. The emphasis is on first-person statements.

I recommend the following communication formula with slight variations. It has worked well over the years. Basically, it has four steps and goes like this:

I feel _____ (if it's not one word, it's not a feeling)

When you _____ (describe the person's behavior, rather than attacking the person)

Because _____ (helps to make sense to the other person why you're having the reaction you're having)

I would like _____ (change your complaint to a request. It's easier to hear. This step is optional.).

Here are a few examples of poor communication followed by effective ways of telling the unarguable truth:

"Barb! You make me crazy [victim stance] with your anxiety about money! Let go, will you?! Just get over it! Practice what you preach with your clients, and deal with that anxiety instead of letting it run you!"

More responsible and effective to say:

"Barb, I'm starting to get frustrated [step one] with your anxiety about money [step two]. I understand money stuff is hard for you [a little bit of understanding never hurts], *and* still [not *but]* it's frustrating, because I start to feel like what I earn is never good enough, yet we're doing fine economically [step three]. Would it help to sit down with our accountant, so we can see, in black and white, how we're doing, and what we can expect down the line [step four]?

Here's another example:

"Drew [Barb's term of endearment for me], you're *never* on time! That's just inconsiderate. When are you going to get it?!"

Better said:

"Drew, I so want our reconnecting at the end of the day to be just that [kindness never hurts], but I first get angry, then just hurt [step one] when you show up late over and over [step two], because [step three] it feels to me [taking responsibility] like I'm at the bottom of your list of things to do. Would you work on that [step four]?"

What follows are some suggestions for improving all of the relationships in your life, not only with life partners, but also with your parents, children, friends, and colleagues. Above all else, the A.R.T. of vital relating demands the courage to be aware, to feel, and to take responsibility for your own happiness.

TRAINING

1. **Review the practice of awareness (Chapter Three).**

2. **Practice telling your partner your internal, unarguable truth in easy situations, simply as a way of becoming known to the other.**

3. **Learn to make all of your statements (except for the description of your partner's behavior) in the first person.**

4. **Be careful not to mix thoughts with feelings. It is of utmost importance that your partner knows your *emotional* truth.**

5. **When you feel yourself being triggered, breathe, pause, and be aware of what is going on inside (feelings, body sensations, perceptions, thoughts, assumptions).**

6. Have the courage to take responsibility for what is going on inside of you. No one makes you feel, think or do anything (unless you're being tortured!).

7. Use the four-step formula above as a start. In time, you'll find your own language, but you would do best to continue to include the four elements of unarguable truth telling.

8. End with a request, rather than blame.

9. Thank your partner for listening. Gratitude is always a great finish.

Chapter 13:

I Like Who I Am With You:
Feelings in Relationships

Simon and Ronald sat on one of their favorite logs by the edge of the water. It was a perfect day in the swamp. The flies and bees hummed peacefully, the willow leaves rustled ever so slightly, and the water trickled past them on its journey through the swamp. And Simon had his best friend right next to him.

"You know," began Simon, "everything seems so right today. I just like how I feel right now. Especially, I like how I feel with you right beside me."

Ronald nodded, but remained quiet for a few moments.

"What're you thinking?" asked Simon, noticing his friend's unusual reticence.

"Remember we were talking the other day, and you said that sometimes I can irritate you?" answered Ronald.

"Yeah," replied Simon. "But that doesn't happen too often, you know."

"Right, but do you like how you feel at times like that? I don't mean irritated or angry or such things. I mean, how you are feeling about you *when I'm irritating you."*

"Ummm, not so good," answered Simon.

"Well, that could be a problem."

*****

The brochure for the workshop that Barbara and I have developed for couples begins as follows:

"I like who I am with you…" was easy to say when you were in love and when life wasn't so complicated, the times when you could remember the best in yourself and appeal to the best in your partner. Holding on to yourself while staying connected, however, is inevitably challenged by conflict, disappointment, and the daily routine of living together…

This chapter explores the tension that results from being an individual *within* a partnership, the central role of vulnerability and integrity, the incessant need to be right, and, finally, the role of emotional honesty in all of these.

Separate and Related

The ultimate dance in relationships has to do with space and togetherness, being separate and connected simultaneously. The musical analogy for this apparently contradictory state is singing harmony, when you must hold onto your own part while listening to and blending with another's.

Kahlil Gibran, in *The Prophet,* advises, "Let there be space in your togetherness…." In his *Letters to a Young Poet*, Rainer Maria Rilke reminds us,

Once the realization is accepted that even between the closest human beings infinite distances continue, a wonderful living side by side can grow, if they succeed in loving the distance between them which makes it possible for each to see the other whole against the sky.

There are two extremes on the continuum of space and connection in relationships. One is the emphasis on being separate, one's own person. The other is a desperate need for connection. The former begets distance and disconnection, the latter, immersion in and confusion with the other.

We need both separation and connection if the relationship is to be a union of equals, both partners strong enough to hold onto themselves and courageous enough to enter the transformative fire of intimacy. David Schnarch, in *Passionate Marriage,* speaks of the marriage as a crucible, the container that keeps a couple together, particularly when things get hot and they are forced to grow up and move beyond their comfort zones. As Schnarch puts it, a relationship is the ultimate "people growing machine."

Kathy and Matt have been dancing in and out of their relationship crucible for years, trying to decide if it's worth all the effort to grow into what they both say they want. Matt is a single parent, raising an eight-year-old daughter, working full time, and looking forward to family life with Kathy. Kathy, on the other hand, divorced for several years, loves having her own space, her own home, yet wants a life with Matt. The more Matt presses her for a commitment, the angrier Kathy gets, blaming Matt's "suffocating" pressure. Matt pursues, and Kathy distances. Matt then explodes out of frustration and helplessness, giving Kathy yet another reason to distance. They had been doing this dance for several years when they finally called me.

"In or out? In or out?" blurted Matt. "Just do one or the other, but don't leave me hanging like this!"

"Well, I *do* want in," replied Kathy. "I just need some space."

"You get tons of space. I want a life together. I'm tired of feeling like a camper in your place on the weekends when you finally get time for us!"

It was clear who did the separating and who tended to pursue. They both were operating primarily out of fear, the emotional backdrop to most relationships.

"Matt," I said, "it seems to me that you're waiting for something from Kathy for you to be happy. I'm wondering if you would be willing to take over the responsibility for your own happiness."

"I'm not sure what you mean."

"The more you push, the more Kathy retreats. Are you willing to do this dance forever?"

"No way."

"Then you'll have to do something different. Be clear as to how much longer you're willing to live apart like this. Kathy might see that as a threat on your part, but you would be taking care of yourself. She might step up to the plate, or she might decide to leave, but in either case, you wouldn't be repeating this tiresome loop."

Both grew quiet. They were clearly afraid.

Matt pursued Kathy so as not to feel like a failure, someone not good enough. His greatest fear was being on his own, standing on his own. Kathy distanced to keep from facing the anxiety of being smothered and without complete freedom of choice. She mostly feared getting lost in and hurt by closeness.

Matt needed to set a limit to Kathy's withdrawing. He needed to risk losing the relationship; otherwise he would remain a hostage to it. Kathy had to face her fear of being drowned in closeness.

Their emotional radar was telling them that continuing the same course would leave Matt feeling like less of a man and Kathy feeling incomplete. Their emotions were also pointing to what was keeping them from moving forward, namely the fear of thinking I'm not good enough, trapped and powerless--feelings triggered by false beliefs. If they were to have a successful relationship, they would have to face these feelings and challenge the false perceptions that set them in motion. Above all, they would have to face the fear that they wouldn't be able to handle these emotions.

As discussed in the previous chapter, recognizing, examining and telling the unarguable truth about one's feelings is the only way to resolve such an impasse. What usually prevents this are three patterns.

The first is the fear of feeling. We cringe at the thought of experiencing fear, shame, anxiety. The solution lies in having the courage to feel, the wisdom to question the false beliefs--I can't live without someone or I can't be too close to anyone-- that drive the feelings, and the strength to step beyond one's comfort zone.

In order to be whole, we need to stand on our own two feet in a context of connectedness. This is the wholeness at the heart of integrity. It is coming home to all that we can be. Not just separate. Not just connected. But both. Not defended and right, but known to and understood by each other. And as two people become known to each other, love prevails.

Two other patterns contributing to the impasse preventing relational honesty are the fear of vulnerability and the need to be right.

Vulnerability as Empowerment

The closer we get to another, the greater the possibility of getting hurt. Often have I heard people tell me that they will never open up because they've been hurt enough. They're not going to get set up again. So they build walls or go on the attack. In either case, they soon discover how lonely it can be, making sure that no one ever gets through to where they can do emotional damage. There's no damage, and there's no connection.

Unable to tolerate the early death of her father whom she had adored, Amanda learned to survive by being tough, a strategy modeled to perfection by her mother, who had worked full time while caring for her husband as he struggled with cancer. The thought of her dam breaking would bring her to the edge of panic. It had always been that way.

Amanda's life evolved into a series of quick relationships in which she felt the early excitement of deeper connection, but bolted quickly, aided by drugs and Johnny

Walker. She amassed a track record of broken hearts and broken agreements.

"So why are you here?" I asked her at our first session.

"I can't seem to hold onto a good relationship. They just don't work for me."

They didn't work because, since her father's death and the overwhelming pain it had caused her, she had made the unconscious decision to close down. She hadn't been hurt since then, but she was lonely as hell.

The Latin root of the word "vulnerable" means the capacity to be wounded. Standard interpretations of this word are shot through with a sense of weakness. In relationships, I find it to be quite the opposite. In order for intimacy to increase, one must be willing to open the doors to very sensitive and, often, wounded parts of ourselves, places we have kept shut to make sure we don't get hurt any more. We have to be strong enough to take the disappointment and hurt if our partner doesn't respond to our opening the way we would like them to. One must be courageous enough to take this step, otherwise walls and locked doors remain in place, and true intimacy continues to be unreachable.

I kept pressing Amanda to pay attention to whatever she was experiencing as we talked.

"Why do you keep asking me the same damned question? It's getting to be a real pain in the ass!"

Tough Lady was out front.

"Because you continue to do the same damned thing with whatever you're feeling," I answered. She looked taken aback. "You try to look tough on the outside, but I think you're scared to death on the inside. You don't look at me, but just stay behind that wall...where it's really lonely. How long has it been lonely for you? And do you want it to go on forever?"

Her eyes briefly met mine. They were softening for the first time in our exchange.

"I'm just so afraid...I don't think I can take all that pain. And for you to see it..."

For the first time since she was a young girl, Amanda was beginning to allow an opening in the closed room of her heart.

Fear and anxiety are the emotional signals that act as sentinels, protecting us from feeling wounded, disappointed, abandoned, and smothered. As long as we avoid these emotions or cover them up with a false front of strength or toughness, we are being driven by that fear. We pretend to be strong, but are, in fact, on very shaky ground. We are pretending to be invulnerable, because underneath it all we are convinced that we really can't take the hit if we are hurt again.

I'm not suggesting that we set ourselves up for hurt and pain, just as I wouldn't suggest standing in the way of an oncoming freight train. I am suggesting that true strength comes from being willing to open the doors to our vulnerability when someone has earned that privilege and when we know that we can deal with whatever happens. Someone earns the privilege of being allowed through the door into where we live emotionally when his/her track record of integrity and honesty is intact. We know we can deal with whatever arises emotionally, if we have been practicing the four steps and have been developing our own emotional competence.

Now we are no longer pretending, constantly on guard and vigilant lest we become mortally wounded again. We are on the firm ground of emotional honesty, listening to when it feels right to open up to someone and knowing that if they don't come through for us, we can handle it and learn from it. At the same time, we are encouraged by the potential reward of greater intimacy.

In all such exchanges, it is our emotions, supported by clear questioning, that encourage us to take a risk or not. Will I most likely grow from a decision to open up? Will such a decision, regardless of outcome, make me stronger? The excitement of possibilities arises. Is this person to be trusted? My fear says not. If not, are my perceptions accurate, my assumptions checked out? Or is it the influence of past pain holding me back when I might take a chance? Attend to the feelings, check out the perceptions and the messages, and then act or not. It's as simple, yet as transformative, as that.

GUIDELINES: Vulnerability or Not

- *LISTEN to the* excitement *about and the* desire *for connection. It is your guidance system at work.*

- *When* fear *arises, don't assume anything. PAY ATTENTION AND CHECK THINGS OUT (Step 3).*

- *ACT: Be clear as to why you don't open up. Make it a choice, not a habit.*

- **ACT: Or open up, even after you've checked out the fear and some trepidation remains. As Susan Jeffers writes, "Feel the fear and do it anyway!"**

Until we bring our unarguable emotional truth into our relationships, we will most likely remain stuck in defending, attacking, blaming, distancing. It's impossible for us, and therefore our relationships, to grow if we don't bring all of who we are into the encounter. We simply are not present without emotional honesty. Matt, Kathy and Amanda all created a great deal of pain by ignoring or being unaware of their feelings. They weren't able to connect to themselves or others, since they hadn't come home to their own emotional truth, the truth that might have set them free.

The term "integrity" has as its root the Latin word for "whole" or "one". Without emotional honesty, we are not whole, we are not in our integrity, not if we are burying, disowning or simply unaware of the very guidance system that tells us how we are doing in the world in general, and in our relationships in particular. Integrity, in my understanding of the word, includes the obvious element of not lying. It also requires a balance and integration of all aspects of an individual (mental, emotional, physical, spiritual). Finally, it refers to the activation of the best in each of us, the fullest expression of who we were meant to be which, additionally, is also the definition of existential freedom, the freedom of full Being.

The Need to Be Right

The insistence on being right and making our partner wrong, is at the heart of many failed marriages. When we are attached to being right, we are in a state of codependence. We need the other to agree with us in order to feel secure and positive about ourselves. We sometimes find it intolerable to allow differences of opinion. This inability reveals itself not only in relationships between people, but between religions and countries as well. Throughout history into our present time, lives have been sacrificed to the gods of inflexibility.

Why do we need to be right and fear being wrong? We've only to listen to the emotional signals (Steps One and Two) and to check out the messages that accompany them (Step Three) to find the answer. This is usually where awareness of the layering of emotions comes into play, as well as the requirement for the unarguable truth.

When the insistence on being right arises, when we feel ourselves digging our heels into a position and when a fear or anxiety appears at the prospect of being wrong, there are several questions that can bring clarity to our emotional responses. "What would I be feeling and believing about myself if I stopped insisting on being right?" "If I were wrong?" "If my partner didn't see it my way?" Often there are beliefs derived from past experiences that make being wrong something to be avoided at all costs.

Jamie and Georgia wanted to get out of the incessant arguing they had experienced since the beginning of their marriage. After they described their dilemma, I asked each of them about their upbringing.

Jamie began. Every desire and every decision he ever made was criticized and questioned by his parents, his father in particular. So Jamie learned to keep his desires and wants to himself. At other times, when his anger and frustration had built up, he would explode at his father's incessant need to be right and to make Jamie wrong.

He remembered an incident after he'd begun middle school that was typical. He had told his father he wanted an English racer rather than an American-made bicycle. "Why a foreign bike? Something wrong with your own country?" his father demanded.

When he met Georgia, Jamie was drawn to someone with a critical edge and a need to be in control of her environment. To some extent, he married his father. In an argument about how to arrange dishes in the dishwasher, Jamie would explode when Georgia rearranged his work.

"It's not such a goddamned big deal!! Would you just let things be for once?!" he'd shout.

"Well, if it's not such a big deal, then why are you getting so worked up? I'm just trying to be a bit more efficient!"

The more Jamie tried to change Georgia's approach, the more she dug in. Loss of control was not something Georgia was comfortable with, given her history of parental criticism, as well as inherited anxiety.

Jamie might have been more successful if he had been emotionally honest with his wife.

He might have said, "When you try to improve on what I'm doing, I get angry, because, for one thing, it's as if you don't appreciate that I'm trying to help out. And, honestly, it hurts a bit. Like it's never good enough."

If Georgia had heard that, she might have understood her husband a bit more, and have begun to value his emotions and sense of self more than her need for efficiency. When understanding becomes more important than being right, the relationship is finally on its way out of being stuck.

Georgia had her own work cut out for herself. If she stopped insisting on being right, she might have to reveal her anxiety about not having things under her control, and underneath that anxiety lay the fear of not being good enough, of not being perfect.

The only way out of the quandary Jamie and Georgia had created for themselves was to enter the truthful and vulnerable levels of emotion, and then to employ the A.R.T. of emotional honesty. That strategy had the potential to make them free to be the best and most courageous version of themselves and to truly connect with each other. Connected rather than right.

You become capable of saying and meaning "I like who I am with you," not because you speed up my heartbeat and give me tingles all the time, not because you agree with me, not because you say what I want to hear, and not because you're always reliable and sensitive. Whether you're acting like a jerk or a saint, it matters not. When I am strong in my integrity, and when I take full responsibility for my well being, I will be happy, regardless of what you say or do.

When I'm with you, I like who I am, regardless.

Chapter 14:

Sweet Sorrow: The Pain of Touch

"Why are you confused?" asked Ronald, as he and Simon moved through the tall, summer grass. The sun was setting behind the edge of the marsh, accompanied by a chorus of bullfrogs, tree frogs, and crickets.

"I'm not sure," replied Simon, "but evenings are the worst. Especially when we're near my old shell." Simon nodded his head to the left, where his empty turtle shell lay, overgrown with brush and moss. "I get really sad, but then sort of relieved and even a bit excited. Then the sadness again. Very confusing."

Ronald always had an answer. Socrates of the swamp. "Do you remember what it was like the first few times I had to be away for a few days to take care of some things at the far end of the marsh? How sad you were? And how glad you were that we had become such good friends?"

"Yeah, like sad and glad at the same time."

"Right," said Ronald. "Sometimes it works like that."

"But what does that have to do with my shell...and the evening?" asked Simon.

"What's it like when you think of your shell and of your life in the shell?"

"Well, that's confusing, too," answered Simon. "It was an ending and a beginning. The ending was scary, and

also a bit sad, because I was there for so long. It was like losing an old friend."

"Any other reason why it might be sad to think of all those years in the shell?"

"Oh, yes, all that time not painting. Just listening to what my mother told me to do."

Ronald continued. "And when you think of finally leaving the shell, what does your radar tell you then?"

"It feels like I escaped, it's exciting."

"There you have it," concluded Ronald, "all at once. Amazing isn't it?"

"But what about the evening part?" asked Simon.

"What happens to the day when evening comes?" asked Ronald, unflappable as usual.

""Oh-h-h," came the reply. "It's over."

"Exactly. And sometimes 'over' is sad and glad at the same time. Isn't it?"

"Now I get it," Simon said. They continued their evening stroll past the old, abandoned shell.

*****

People often wonder why something good, such as a long-awaited hug, can simultaneously feel sad. Shakespeare called it "sweet sorrow." In the moment of parting from a loved one, we feel the power of connection and anticipate the reunion. And the separation hurts. Joy and pain, relief and grief are often emotional bedfellows. Recognizing these apparent emotional contradictions and being with each of the clashing feelings will deepen our understanding of what is, as well as what has or has not been.

Clifford Smith, my mentor of many years, calls this the "pain of touch." The word "touch" here is metaphorical--how we are touched emotionally. Conflicting emotions tend to confuse people, leaving them thinking their emotional system has gone over the edge. It hasn't. It is just giving them several signals at once. Remember that feelings don't always come in neat packages. They are messengers, and at times, the content of the message can be complex.

This pain of touch is different from the confusing emotions that attend situations such as divorce, where grief and relief, anger and fear take turns in the emotional driver's seat. These feelings come in waves that follow closely, one upon the other. When the pain of touch occurs, it is more like two waves crashing against each other at the same time. It is often a bittersweet experience

I was in my first long-term relationship when I was twenty-something. It ended for a number of reasons, but I had also fallen in love with someone else, had told Eve about it, and I simply didn't know what to do. Eve did.

"It's too painful for me to stick around while you try to figure out what you want to do with your relationships."

She left me. For six months, I cried myself to sleep each night. Although it was clear that a committed relationship was not right for us, I felt a deep sadness. All I could do was to sit with the feelings until they finally receded months later.

A year after we broke up, we met up in New York City. The moment that I saw her brought up several feelings: sadness, guilt and, surprisingly, a very deep sense of relief. When we hugged, the tears poured out. I could feel the loss of what was and what was not to be, guilt over having been the instigator of our breakup, and relieved to know that the connection that touched both of us was still intact. How painful and happy was that hug, all in the same moment.

Often when I hug clients at the end of a session, they feel conflicting emotions, and ask, "Why does this hurt so much? It feels so good to be hugged...God, it's been so long."

When a person who has been on an affection starvation diet is hugged or touched, they feel not only the joy of physical connection, but the length of time they have had to do without it. In such moments we need to simply attend to the feelings, all of the feelings. Our guidance system is telling us not only what we've lost, what we've done without, perhaps how we've messed up or what we can no longer look forward to, as well as what feels good and right, and what we need more of in our life.

Tiger Woods won the British Open a couple of days ago. His father, who had mentored him all the years as he mastered the game, had died two months earlier.

"I'm the sort of guy," Tiger said, "who just bottles things up and moves on."

When he made the last putt, winning for the first time in months, a few tears fell. He buried his head in his caddy's shoulder. In his wife's embrace, he finally sobbed. The joy and relief of the win, and the poignant wish that his father had been there all came together at once. A man who is not known for his emotional exuberance screamed a triumphant "Yes!" and then cried a river over his father's absence.

A dear friend, Matthew, struggles with anxiety over finances. Self-employed, his business is sometimes up, sometimes down. He loves what he does, and managed to purchase an impressive Victorian home for his family and his enterprises, which, in turn, added to his anxiety.

One Thanksgiving, just before sitting down to dinner with his wife and two children, he looked out his window to see a homeless man picking through his garbage. The bent figure reached in, found a piece of fruit, and straightened up with a broad grin on his face.

Matthew was struck with deep sadness for this person, fear that he himself could wind up that way, and relief that he was inside a wonderful home with a loving family. And the amazing smile on the face of the homeless man gave Matthew a new perspective on what it means to have or not have.

As Matthew watched this homeless person, and as I encounter such people in my travels, there is often sadness and a sense of warm recognition simultaneously. The sadness has to do with the distance that our different roles and identities create, such as the distance between "successful" and "homeless." And the awareness of how much our lives have been spent in this place of separation.

The recognition, however, is of our *sameness*, with the fact that each of us matters, that each of us hurts, and that each of us seeks--and can find--contentment, as seen in the street person's smile. In that moment, we know the oneness of this web of life of which we are a part. In that moment, we come home once again to who we most truly are. Separate, yet profoundly connected.

This coming together of different feelings can bring a mixture of messages, as well as revelations. Such moments are like treasures washed up by waves of emotions upon our consciousness. These are gifts from the sea, if only we have the courage to receive them.

Chapter 15:

Emotions at Work:
Repeating Family Patterns on the Job

In an era when changing jobs is commonplace, what might keep employees working for the same company year after year? I believe it will have to be the "culture," the environment that workers and management create. It will have to be a culture of integrity, compassion and emotional honesty.

This kind of culture requires consciousness, specifically an awareness of the fact that we bring to our job the same patterns of relating that we learned growing up. Without this awareness, we replay the relational patterns that have followed us like bad dreams since childhood. Without this consciousness, our workplace becomes one, large dysfunctional family, which translates into inefficiency and loss of productivity.

For several years, I was asked to deliver stress management courses at a Fortune 500 company. One day, workers for the company were sitting in a small focus group, helping me get a better sense of whether patterns of emotional dysfunction were being transferred from home to workplace.

"It's not written into any policy," said one woman in her forties, an employee of about twelve years. "It's not even told to you directly. But you just know that you've got to, as they say, leave your emotions at the door when you come to work.

"I mean, I'm not bringing my personal life into work. That wouldn't be good. I understand that. But any show of emotion, especially strong emotion, seems to really upset my bosses (all male, by the way). They just seem to want to make the feelings go away so that they can get on with the business of productivity."

I soon discovered that this was typical. And, it wasn't a new experience for this employee. She had learned to hide many of her feelings growing up, particularly from her father, a career military man who insisted on avoiding emotional displays. She never dared to let him know how she was feeling, something she repeated with her boss. In a word, her work life was a replay of familial patterns, and when you put dysfunctional patterns from many families under one corporate roof, you've got the potential for an unpleasant atmosphere and an inefficient work force.

In families, there is often a fear that becoming "emotional" will get out of control and create chaos. Anxiety is the watchdog, keeping the feared emotions under wraps. It's not much different in workplaces, where the fear is that emotions will get in the way of productivity. But, as with families, denying emotional reality is precisely what divides and damages a workplace.

In the absence of honesty of any kind, a group will suffer, be it a family or a work force. When emotional honesty is not practiced, group members become strangers to each other, and strangers are not as supportive of each other as are people connected through authenticity.

When we were children in our families, we usually didn't have much of a voice. If the grownups modeled emotional avoidance, that's pretty much what we did as well. As adults, however, we have the opportunity to exercise more choice, both at home and at work. The choice is to be emotionally clear and authentic with each other. Simply put, we have the choice to become more real and, in so doing, to create a much healthier and productive environment.

Damage to the workplace is further compounded when employees not only withhold emotional truth, but also make assumptions in the absence of true understanding and knowledge of each other--another pattern learned growing up. They then act as if the assumptions were the truth without checking them out. Recall the power of projection. The less we know about each other, the easier it is to project and blame. Assuming, projecting, and blaming are hallmarks of unhealthy marriages and families, and places of work, as well.

It also goes without saying that personal problems and dilemmas should primarily be dealt with outside the job. We need to learn to put feelings on the back burner, while waiting for the appropriate time and place to deal with them. This is where competent use of Steps One and Two is essential, rather than simply denying the existence of our emotions.

At times, however, it's not that easy to leave personal difficulties at the door, because we don't surgically remove our emotional radar when we go to work.

On such occasions making our feelings known to a trusted co-worker or manager can be a way of reducing the emotional intensity (Step Four), allowing us to redirect our focus back to the job. With respect to personal satisfaction as well as job productivity, emotional self-awareness and sharing is one of the best investments an employee can make in his/her work culture.

BASIC STEPS IN KEEPING THE AIR CLEAR

1. **BE AWARE of what your feelings are indicating**

2. **TAKE RESPONSIBILITY for your perceptions and assumptions.**

3. **If you are perceiving and then assuming some kind of offense, CHECK IT OUT with the other person(s).**

4. **If this doesn't seem "safe," CHECK OUT the reality of your fears.**

5. **If your fears are realistic, then CONSIDER HAVING A THIRD PARTY join the discussion.**

6. **BE THE PERSON you would want to work with.**

In order for a corporate culture to embody emotional competency and integrity, these qualities must be modeled from the top down. Executives and managers themselves become more human and worthy of respect when they are emotionally honest. This is particularly true of male executives and managers, since emotional competence is usually not viewed as a trait of successful male leaders. One of the most moving stories I've ever read with regard to a leader inspiring commitment through emotional authenticity is in the book, *Executive EQ*, by Robert Cooper and Ayman Sawaf.

Robert Cooper had been traveling in Tibet on a research project to study the inner aspects of leadership. He was traveling in the mountains with a guide and a local elder, a leader of his village. They stopped to look over the breathtaking view from a summit, when the elder pointed to a spot in a ravine below and began to tell his story.

In 1959, the Chinese had occupied his country, forbidding the expression of any religious or spiritual belief. The elder was observed one day bowing to a friend he had passed on the road, an ancient way of greeting one another with words that mean, "I honor the greatness in you."

It was decided he had to be punished and made an example of. He was forced to watch his wife and family brutally murdered and tossed into the ravine he now pointed to.

The Chinese then proceeded to destroy one of the wooden bridges that crossed the river to the village, making it very difficult for the villagers to travel back and forth. They told the villagers that they would have to rebuild it themselves, knowing that Tibetans are traditionally fearful of deep water. The elder was then led from the place where his family lay dead to the destroyed bridge and challenged to begin the rebuilding.

The elder could have chosen to retaliate, but made the decision to do the only thing he could. He waded into the waters, picked up a huge stone and carried it to one of the bridge pilings, saying, "I will carry a hundred stones and timbers for each of my lost relatives." The villagers, stunned by this show of courage and determination, joined him, rebuilding the bridge in several months.

The elder had been chosen as the village leader before the Chinese invasion, which prevented him from taking the position. On that day, standing in the water, he assumed his leadership role. He showed, but also managed his feelings, directing the emotional energy in the most redemptive way possible.

As he told his story to Robert, the elder was visibly shaking. But then he turned to Robert and asked, "So tell me about *your* life, Robert." Robert, shaken himself by the story, asked how the elder could let go of the pain and continue their conversation. He replied that the Chinese took everything from him except for two things: "First, what I value and believe—what I *feel*, beneath everything else, is true in my heart, even when my mind can't prove or explain it. And second, short of killing me, they could not take away how I express *who I am* on the path of my destiny. These are the things that make me real and give me hope."

The elder explained to Robert why he needed to reveal his story. "Without knowing this, you do not know me. The deep me, the real me. I could never be a leader of you. And you could not wholeheartedly work beside me or follow me. Now, if you choose to, you can begin to know me, and work with me, and trust me. Now I am real, I am not just a name. I have a heart and a voice and a life story. I am not just some stranger who climbed a mountain with you."

"In Tibet," he continued, "we call this *authentic presence*. It means, literally, 'field of power.' When we live from here, from the inside, we can talk openly and honestly with each other, and say the things we deeply feel...We hold ourselves, and each other, accountable to our best effort in all things..."

This is what I would call extreme authenticity and radical integrity. This is someone I would work with and for. If our leaders cannot model authenticity and integrity for us, it will be all the more difficult for employees to do it on their own.

As children, we played the game, follow the leader. The rules were that you followed the leader blindly. But the leader always had to do the required task first. We seem to have forgotten this childhood lesson to commit to the one who walks the talk. And, of course, as adults, we don't go blindly.

Perhaps not many CEOs and upper management can be as real and transparent as that elder. All of us, from executives to line workers, have our histories and our conditioning. Yet if there is at least more emotional honesty, if emotional truth is not only respected, but encouraged, the work culture will improve tremendously. And it must be modeled at the top so that it can take root among the ranks of employees.

Emotional competence must be encouraged as a way of becoming *more real* and, therefore, *more easily understood and known* to each other. The more inscrutable, mysterious, and distant an executive appears, the less employees will want to commit to his/her company and goals. Being emotionally inscrutable may have been a CEO's way of life growing up, a way to manage and survive. But in the adult work world, it is a path that leads to mistrust and decreased loyalty and commitment.

Jim was the team leader for a group of engineers at that same Fortune 500 company. Even during the most difficult time of the company's downsizing, he always had the loyalty and cooperation of his team members. Like the Velveteen Rabbit, Jim was real with them. He was emotionally open and honest, but was beginning to burn out with the task of taking care of managers who had to fire faithful employees.

I received a call from him one day, asking if I could spend a few hours with his managers.

"Just give them something to work with. They're really hurting."

So was he.

I agreed, and met with his group for several hours, first helping to identify the negative beliefs and emotions that were plaguing them.

"I'm letting people down," came one voice.

"I've got this knot in my stomach all the time," said another.

"I'm just furious that it had to happen this way! They dug the hole, and now our people have to pay for it," someone said.

As we went around the table, Jim finally spoke.

"I just feel this sadness, kind of a helplessness. It's with me a lot, even messing up my sleep at night."

Heads nodded around the table.

Now we had some things to work with. Over time, Jim had created an atmosphere of openness, of honesty. The very act of being aware of (Step One) and choosing to reveal beliefs and emotions (Step Four) enabled us to move forward. At times, there is little we can do other than feel our feelings (Step Two), but to do that can be an enormous relief, particularly if it can be done in a supportive community of co-workers.

It was also critical that the messages of the feelings be checked out (Step Three).

"I just feel so guilty all the time, having to tell people they don't have a job. This morning I had to let go a husband and his wife. They were invited to move here with promises of great jobs, etc. So we've uprooted them, gotten them to come here, they bought a huge home, and now we're firing them."

This person's belief was that he should be doing something and that somehow the firing was his fault (guilt's message: I *may* have violated someone). Once clear about the presence of the feeling and its message, he could begin to challenge the false beliefs. Once the guilt passed, he was able to step up to the task of facing the helplessness and sadness that Jim had described. This "facing" is not a passive surrender. It is "being with" the emotion, so that it can move through, rather than be buried, which only adds to stress, burnout, and an inability to cope.

The challenge is to be with what *really is,* rather than hide it. We spend a great deal of energy burying emotions. Feelings are physical energy, and it takes energy to hold them down, even when we're unconscious of that process. This repression drains us and disconnects us, particularly if it is modeled at the top of the corporate hierarchy.

Problems arise at work when emotions and assumptions are shoved under the table. Jim supported his team in placing emotions and assumptions on the table, where the light of honesty and courage was able to lift some of the heavy cloud that sat over them. The openness enlivened them and reconnected them to themselves and each other, enabling them to be more available to their employees.

With reference to the workplace, it can be said that *it's all about you*. It is the individual, whether employee, manager or executive, who must take on the responsibility for creating an authentic and life-giving culture at the job.

EXECUTIVE AND MANAGERIAL TASKS

1. **BE THE LEADER you would want to work for.**

2. **WALK THE TALK. One of the most demoralizing experiences in any workplace is a double standard.**

3. **TELL THE TRUTH, which includes avoiding making promises or predictions that may not materialize.**

4. **IF YOU DON'T KNOW, say "I don't know."**

5. **BE AS EMOTIONALLY HONEST as you can, and not only when you're angry or frustrated, but also when you're pleased and excited.**

6. **BE REAL. Avoid roles and masks.**

7. **REMEMBER that each person working for you has feelings, values, hopes, and fears. Address the WHOLE PERSON, not just his/her productivity potential.**

Other things we learned at home and bring to work

Rigidity, the need to be right, is another damaging trait driven by fear and a need to self-protect that interferes with understanding and being understood. As in marriages, the need to be right often supercedes the need to understand and to be understood. How many conflicts at work might be avoided or resolved if the parties involved were emotionally honest and committed to understanding, rather than being right?

The more we need to guard and hide our feelings or need to be right, the more the conflictual pattern will arise, like the complaining husband and wife who have the same argument over and over. Instead, if we focus on being emotionally honest and on knowing and being known, energy is freed up, we feel lighter and more connected, and work productivity soars of its own accord.

How were conflicts typically dealt with as we grew up? For many of us, very little emotional awareness was ever employed to resolve issues. Instead, there was the insistence on winning the argument and being right.

Similarly, in the workplace certain skills, often referred to as conflict management, are taught to enable employees to resolve disagreements. Unfortunately, there is usually very little attention in these trainings to emotional courage and competence. Skills can be taught but are of little help without *awareness* (of emotions and assumptions) plus *responsibility* plus *truth telling* (remember: A+R+T=Vital Relationship).

The title of the workshop that I bring to businesses in need of conflict resolution and change management is "Community *Through* Conflict." It is based upon the cornerstones of awareness, integrity, and vital relationship. These come first, before learning the "tools" of communication and conflict resolution.

In advice columns and articles for business people having to deal with change, I've often read about the "Four Ways" or "Seven Steps" in mastering change. Never have I come across the necessity of becoming aware of one's anxiety, having the courage to feel, reveal and manage it. This, I believe, is partially the result of how we learned (or didn't learn) to resolve conflicts growing up.

Mike's co-worker, George, was giving a presentation about time management. Mike told me later that "in front of all those people," George said that for some, this was an innately difficult task, and looked directly at Mike. Indignant and feeling discredited in public, Mike was furious. When he came to see me, he was still angry and enjoyed being at work less and less.

The solution was really simple but demanded courage. If he felt angry, then his feelings were telling him that he *may* have been violated. But he needed to check it out, not only to prevent it from happening again (if, in fact, that was the case), but to release the burden of the stored anger that was making his experience at work generally unpleasant. Stockpiled anger quickly devolves into resentment and bitterness, a very burdensome yolk to bear.

Mike not only had neglected to check out his perceptions, but he wasn't paying attention to how *familiar* these feelings of being singled out and embarrassed were. He grew up with them, living with his mother who put the wicked witch of the West to shame. He married a critical woman and was now convinced that he had experienced it at work.

These old reactions or sore spots cannot simply be left at the door to our workplace. This is the process of projection that each of us enters into unknowingly from time to time. Our past hurtful experience, stored behind some neurological wall in our brains, kicks in like a movie when we experience anything similar in the present. In Mike's case, George was the projection screen.

In another example, Sol was a bright star in the engineering department of his corporate workplace. He was so competent at the projects he was given and so well connected to the coworkers under his leadership that upper management entertained high expectations for him. Sol knew this and proceeded to drive himself to meet those expectations, just as he had growing up with professional parents who expected great things of their children.

He made the mistake of not listening to the fear and anxiety that drove his behavior, which made it impossible to recognize the belief ("I *must* be the best") that set everything in motion. He soon found his marriage on very shaky grounds. "We're your family," his wife would say, "but we're way down on your priority list!"

Sol began to inexplicably suffer panic attacks. He had created an impossible situation for himself. He somehow magically thought he could pour himself completely into his job and still have all the necessary time to be a husband and a father.

Josh, on the other hand, could never get his work done on time. It was always of superior quality but never met the deadline. His boss continuously pushed him to move more quickly and let go of his need to do everything perfectly. Yet, when he tried to do an "okay job," his guilt and shame would go off. Instead of dealing with and examining the messages behind his feelings, he remained compulsively perfect...and lost his job. "Never good enough" was the motto branded upon his brain as he grew up, and he would do anything and everything perfectly, even to the point of losing his job, to avoid having those feelings again.

Emotional intelligence and emotional competence are an investment that inevitably lead to wonderful returns in any business, because a business' greatest asset—its employees—will be working in an atmosphere of emotional honesty and interpersonal integrity. In such a milieu, a sort of corporate androgyny unfolds in which masculine efficiency and feminine connectedness join forces to create the workplace of our dreams.

When management displays honesty, it earns respect and loyalty. When co-workers create an atmosphere of honesty and openness modeled by management, they create a culture of mutual support, productivity, and positive feeling. When employers and employees become emotionally competent enough to avoid repeating old and dysfunctional patterns of behavior at work, they begin to discover personal peace, empowerment and productivity. The bottom line is an extraordinary win-win.

Chapter 16:

Guilt, Shame, Pride and Self-esteem

In the midst of winter I finally learned there was in me an invincible summer.

Albert Camus

A strange sight greeted Ronald one morning. He was passing the place where Simon had left his turtle shell. Ronald was used to glancing at it to see how overgrown it had become. He always grinned at the thought of how far Simon had come since their first meeting. Today, when he looked at it, however, he saw a sight he was not likely to forget.

Simon was beside his old shell, and it looked as if he was trying to get back in. His head was buried inside the shell, the rest of his body sticking out.

"Simon, buddy," exclaimed Ronald, "what's going on!? You trying to get back into that shell?"

"No!" came Simon's muffled voice from inside the shell. "I'm just hiding."

Ronald chuckled. "Well, it's not your best side that I'm seeing, big guy, and it's hard to miss."

"This is not funny. Not funny at all!"

"So what's going on?" repeated Ronald.

"I did something terrible last evening. Really bad!" said Simon.

"What did you do that was so bad?"

"You know how I get frustrated with the bullfrogs," said Simon, *as he slowly extracted his head from the shell,* *"and their noisy voices when I'm trying to paint?"*

"Yeah."

"Well, last evening I couldn't take it any more. I threw my paints and brushes into their pond, completely messing up where they live. Then I screamed at them, over and over. They finally shut up, but ..."

"But what?" asked Ronald.

"I could see their faces," Simon went on. "Even the baby frogs. They all looked scared. And they couldn't get into the water with the paint in it. I feel just awful. So I'm hiding my face so no one can see me."

"Yep, not good," replied Ronald. "But what's hiding your head going to do?"

"I just don't want anyone to see me," said Simon. "They must think I'm the worst turtle in the swamp."

"Maybe, but that doesn't make it so."

"But I am *horrible!" said Simon.*

"Well, doing bad and being bad aren't the same thing," replied Ronald impatiently, "in case I've never put it to you that way."

"But I feel *so bad!" exclaimed Simon.*

"But remember, how you **feel** *is not who you* **are***. You'll always be absolutely fine, even when you blow it!"*

"Well, then how do I get this feeling to quit? It's killing me!"

"It might let up if you stop beating up on yourself, get your head out of the shell, and do something different to

make it up to the frogs," said Ronald. "Hiding your head won't get you anywhere, and it won't fix the pond."

*****

We are born to feel good about ourselves. It's as instinctual as a flower leaning towards the light, yet it can be the hardest thing to accomplish.

As we have seen thus far, our emotions guide us, energize, and connect us. During our entire journey, we yearn for and lean towards who we most authentically are. We are always heading Home, whether we are conscious of it or not.

During this journey, certain emotions can be challenging, particularly given the false messages that set them in motion. These feelings are guilt, shame and pride.

We leave the home of our childhood to come Home to who we truly are, who we were born to be. Beyond definitions and images of who we believe we "should" be lies the land of the "true Self," as therapists would call it, or our Christ or Buddha nature as Christians or Buddhists would describe it. It is a glorious journey, an exciting undertaking, yet it is replete with dungeons and dragons ready to imprison us with fears and false goals.

This is the journey that T.S. Eliot refers to when he writes: "We shall not cease from exploration, and the end of all our exploring will be to arrive where we started and know the place for the first time." It is the meeting with our deepest and most authentic nature, which Rumi describes: "Out beyond ideas of wrongdoing and rightdoing, there is a field. I will meet you there."

It looks something like this:

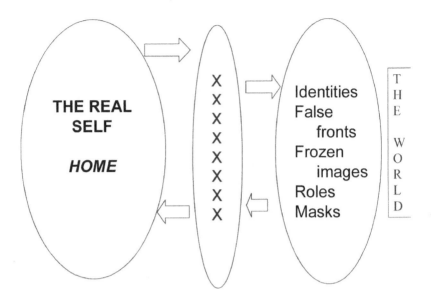

We are conceived in a wonderful state of perfection, in the bliss of the womb, connected to everything around us *(the real Self/Home)*. I intentionally mention conception and not physical birth, since by the time we've spent nine months or so in our mother's womb, we have already picked up much of mom's emotional baggage. We are physically born, begin to grow through infancy and childhood, and inevitably experience negative moments in which we begin to doubt or forget the perfect start we had.

We subsequently take on negative beliefs *(the x's inside of the middle figure)* about ourselves as a result of early relationships and experiences. These beliefs are false stories we tell ourselves about ourselves. These stories, when wired to emotions and body sensations, become extremely powerful and drive the image-making machine that creates the masks we don (*Identities, false fronts, etc*) in order to keep the world from seeing the negative stuff that we've come to believe is our true nature.

Dismantling these stories and masks, however, entails having the courage to deal with the painful emotions that accompany these early experiences and beliefs.

Foremost among these emotional challenges is the toxic form of shame, which is driven by the false belief that *who we are* is intrinsically flawed and damaged. It is the fear of feeling this shame that intimidates so many because it brings us into contact with a sullied image of ourselves. It's the feeling that makes us want to cover our face and hide.

Typically, these false self-images are formed in childhood. We then live our adolescent and adult lives as if they were true, limiting our possibilities, finding it difficult to take in anything positive, even so much as a compliment.

As a young boy of five, George lived outside a town in West Virginia with his parents, who farmed for a living. Given the spaciousness around their home, George would at times have a group of playmates over to play games in the open fields.

On one particular July morning, a perfect day for childhood games and fantasy, George had several friends over to play hide and seek. So engrossed was he in the game, that he forgot to pay attention to his body signals and released a bowel movement, soiling both his underwear and the shorts he was wearing. Telltale, murky-colored streams of release appeared on his bare legs.

His friends began to jeer and taunt. Worst of all, his mother, upon hearing the teasing, looked to see what was taking place, and when she did, grabbed George by the arm, spun him around, and shouted, "I *told* you," she roared, "to pay attention to when you needed to go to the bathroom. You're not a baby anymore! Or are you!?"

Totally humiliated, George was dragged inside the house to change. The game was over, but his life of shame had just begun. At a very high price, he would make sure that he never let his shit show again.

Connie was born to parents who were usually too stoned to know how to care for a child. Very quickly, they decided to give Connie up for adoption. She was adopted by a couple who divorced by the time she was three, partially due to the mother's alcoholism and the father's unrelenting criticism. Mother remarried another critical partner, who demonized her sexual development.

By the time Connie was twelve, she was pumped with antidepressants, was cutting herself for emotional relief, and starving herself for some sense of control in her life. She was convinced that she would never be good enough for anyone to stay with her or to approve of her.

Joey was thirty-something when he came to see me, but his problems and self-doubt began in the seventh grade. He had been surrounded by nuns, his mother who was raising him and his sister by herself, and by Holy Mother, the Church. Without knowing it at the time, he was afraid to be seen as attractive, particularly as sexy, since falling into the trap of physical attraction was tantamount to mortal sin and led to an eternity in hell. As a teenager, if he felt attractive or felt his adolescent hormones draw him towards some plaid-skirted Catholic girl, he was immediately convinced that he was intrinsically bad.

Whether the message was "Don't let anyone see your shit!", "You're not worth sticking around for!," or "It's wrong to be sexy!," the outcome was the same for each of these examples: the sense of Self as good, worthy, exciting, and to be celebrated was left behind.

These anecdotes reflect clear cases of experiencing Self-denial and shame, even though nothing bad was done. The situation is more difficult when someone actually has done something wrong according to his/her own values and ethics. Remember that guilt lets us know that we *may* have done something wrong, and it's important to listen to this signal to make sure we're not violating others or our own principles. Guilt exists to teach us, not to punish or shame us. Yet, the slope between guilt and shame is a very slippery one. Behaving wrongly easily becomes being wrong.

April's marriage was pretty much a disaster. She was intimidated by her husband's temper and criticism. They had two children when April became pregnant again. Her husband insisted on an abortion. Although it went against her beliefs and her desires, she was afraid to disagree. She had the abortion. For the next several years, April tried to regain a sense of control in her life, as well as atone for her abortion by restricting her food intake. Eventually she became anorexic. When I met her, she was five feet, six inches tall and weighed ninety pounds.

April's guilt had quickly devolved into shame. Unable to deal directly with the shame, she blamed it on her body. Her flesh became the scapegoat. If she could keep weight off her bones, she would avoid feeling the shame. She had not only *done* something wrong, but now *was* wrong in her very being. She was bad.

We can't undo past mistakes or poor choices, but there are two things we can do. First, we can neutralize and correct the stories about our past experiences that tie us to these false self-perceptions. Secondly, we can take opportunities to build up the positive inside us. We can notice when guilt and shame are driven by false messages, and we can feed healthy pride and self-esteem.

Pride often conjures up images of arrogance and boastfulness. However, Nathaniel Brandon, in *The Six Pillars of Self Esteem,* defines pride and self-esteem as follows: "Pride is the emotional reward of achievement…. Self-esteem contemplates what needs to be done and says 'I can'. Pride contemplates what has been accomplished and says 'I did'." The "I can" of self-esteem is the result of a number of things including achievements, positive input from significant people in our life, and finally, the alignment of our values and behaviors--what I call the "chiropractic life." Before self-esteem and pride can flourish, however, one must deal with toxic shame.

Here's a brief summary:

What is it?

> *Toxic shame* is the emotional response to a perception, thought, or belief that there is something intrinsically wrong with me as a person, that who I am is defective.
> *Healthy shame* reminds me that I have limits and that others have rights and boundaries. I don't have the right to play God.

Toxic shame and guilt differentiated:

Guilt - what I *did* was wrong.

Shame - who I *am* is wrong.

Sources of toxic shame:

Family of origin, society, relationships, work, self

Remember: An inverse ratio exists between toxic shame and self-esteem.

Shame (its toxic form) is, literally, a Self-killer. But, as with all feelings, it is doing its job. It is telling us that something *may* be wrong with who we are. The problem is the false belief or Self-perception that drives it. Where do we get these false beliefs? What are the shame-builders in our lives?

Childhood abuse in any form is one of the most pernicious shame-builders. The abused child is left with the belief that there is something damaged or dirty about him or her. The young ego is not established enough to place the blame where it belongs.

Yet even without abuse, we have all been put down, criticized in a way that was not helpful or constructive, but was delivered out of malice or frustration. This is one of the most common forms of shame-building. Men, in their need to be seen as competent, adequate, and strong, often experience toxic shame when their knowledge or competency is questioned. Women often experience shame when they are not approved of as loving, sensitive, and self-sacrificing. In addition to things said and done to us in childhood (acts of commission), negative Self-beliefs can develop in an environment of omission, as when the basic love and support that we need from our parents are missing.

This can occur in school and the workplace when accomplishments aren't acknowledged.

Another contributor to toxic shame is our inner critic, the monitor of our interior world. This is the harsh, inner voice that criticizes and reprimands us. Some may call it the superego, others our internal gremlins. Although its purpose is to help us avoid getting into trouble, it can become a rigid dictator, driven by a childhood fear of being shamed again. *In its fear of more shame, it criticizes us to keep us in line. In so doing, however, it adds to the shame-based stockpile.*

When Joey, for example, entered his sexual potency in his twenties, he carried the critical voice that had been formed in his childhood Catholic environment. The voice would kick in, telling him his sexual interests were bad (guilt) and that he was bad for entertaining them (shame).

How can we deal with these shame-builders? *First, acknowledge and feel the feeling.* We do all sorts of things *not* to feel shame. We work harder, fall in line more, drink and drug more, dress up to look good, have our bodies surgically altered. In a word, we kill our Selves, and, at times, we kill others emotionally (marriages) and physically (crime and war), to keep from feeling our shame.

Second, check the reality of the message connected with the feeling. The message of toxic shame is *always* false. For my theistic readers, remember that "God don't make no junk." For those of an atheistic or agnostic bent, if, as Camus suggests, you create your meaning and purpose in life, then which belief do you choose to support: "I'm bad, hopeless and helpless in a world that sucks anyway," or "I can choose to be and do good in a world that sorely needs both"?

We are not only intrinsically good, I believe, but we have the potential to be powerful and love-driven creators of good things. Whatever we focus on will grow. In standing up to toxic shame and, more accurately, the beliefs that trigger it, we must have the courage to face and transform the Self-concepts that we have often inadvertently and always erroneously accepted.

Third, share the feeling with someone who will not judge you, someone whose eyes do not feel shaming. Isolation feeds shame. Be conscious of the false beliefs and recall more positive and Self-supportive ones, and live by them. Take action and be what you believe by becoming aware of how you defend against the experience of shame and by then changing your behaviors.

WHAT TO DO ABOUT SHAME ATTACKS

1. **Acknowledge and feel the feeling.**

2. **Reality check the message connected with the feeling: "I'm bad, defective, etc."**

3. **Reveal the feeling of shame to someone who will not judge you.**

4. **Be aware of how you defend against or compensate for the feeling of shame.**

5. **Change your behaviors, particularly co-dependent ones, by listening to what is right for you in every situation and living from the inside out, not vice-versa. This is *integrity*.**

---

6. Explore the source of your shame-based beliefs and do some housecleaning.

As your Self-esteem grows (I can do it), it feeds a healthy pride (I did it). Pride then supports Self-esteem, until we have created a positive cycle of growth and productivity.

What are some of the pride-builders that can offset the influence of the shame-builders? I begin with a brief review of integrity, defined in three ways. First, integrity is saying what you mean and doing what you say. It occurs when your behaviors line up with your values. Secondly, integrity is a sense of wholeness or integration, when your relationships, work, mind, body, emotions, and spirit all line up and are in harmony or balance. This is the chiropractic life. Finally, integrity can be viewed as "following one's bliss," as Joseph Campbell described it. It is the full commitment to that for which we have passion, that which makes our hearts sing.

The greater the presence of integrity in all of its forms in our life, the more at peace we are, the greater our pride in who we are, and the greater our Self-esteem. In the state of integrity, it is our true Self that is calling the shots; not a self based on fear in need of approval or control. When we live from Being, our doing and having flow from this congruency and bring us satisfaction. Integrity is what makes for a great night's sleep.

Another pride builder is recognizing and letting go of the need for unhealthy control *without shame*. As unlikely as it sounds, we need to learn to feel bad, to lose, to make mistakes, and be disappointed without creating a false and unnecessary story about the world or ourselves. If I feel sad, for example, shame views this as weakness. Healthy pride, however, honors the need and the courage to acknowledge loss. If I make a mistake or lose a tennis match or disappoint someone, shame translates this as defective or deficient. Pride knows I am a work in progress, continually unfolding.

April had to learn the lesson that guilt over having an abortion brought to her: not to allow fear of someone's reactions to cause her to abandon her own values. Then it was time for regret, which is close to grief, wishing it could have been different. Healthy grief and regret, having the courage to face something we can't control or change, will guide us towards resolution and new learning, rather than a shameful self-image.

Pride will also increase when we consciously listen to our emotional radar about the balance between our Self-care, relationships to others and our jobs. Stress, particularly in the form of frustration, irritation, depression, burnout and anxiety, signals that we are out of balance, out of alignment, and no longer in our integrity. When our life is in harmony, pride increases, and we just feel good about who we are and what we are doing.

In other words, look to how you are feeling about yourself before wondering how others are reacting to you. Easier said than done, I'll admit, but necessary. And the first step is always awareness, noticing whether I'm connecting with a person or experience from the inside out, or the other way around.

Finally, keep track of successes. It might help to keep some sort of success journal. This suggestion is usually where my male clients chuckle, when they would most likely prefer to gag. But it works. Read over your list every couple of days and notice the progress. It helps you stay out of the old stories.

Overcoming shame and building Self-esteem is a lifelong journey. I recall one client, upon her first visit to the office, asking, "I want to know who I am." This was such a crucial question, one that would eventually lead her past the false, shame-based identities back to her "true nature." I said to her, "First, learn what your feelings are telling you, then learn to answer the question, 'What do I want?', and finally, act on it. It's as simple and as profound as that."

First, what do I want? Then what do others want? First, where am I going? Then how am I going to get there? First, what fits and is right for me? Then how does this fit into the world around me? Asking these questions in the wrong order is asking for trouble.

What follows are a few personal training exercises to help you recognize and deal with shame builders, while increasing the pride builders in your life.

SHAME BUILDERS I HAVE KNOWN

- **Recall the last time you experienced toxic shame and low esteem.**

- **What were the negative self-beliefs that were part of that experience?**

- Let those feelings and negative beliefs be a bridge to times in your past when you experienced similar feelings

- What was the event? Who was involved? Was shame triggered by commission or omission? What did you tell yourself as a result?

- Where in your present life do you experience shame and low esteem? Home? Relationships? Work? Society? (Be specific)

- Pick one or two of these present occurrences and strategize how you might deal with them.

PRIDE-BUILDERS I HAVE KNOWN

Do the above exercises, with the exception of the last suggestion. Instead, strategize how you might increase the presence of pride-building people and events in your life and *how you might in turn become a pride-builder for others.*

Chapter 17:

Handling Change, Tough Decisions, and Addictive Patterns

"Success is never final, and failure is never fatal. It's courage that counts."

Author unknown

"But I never did anything like that before," said Simon about his throwing paints and brushes into the frog pond. "I just can't go back there." Simon imagined the terror of going back to the pond and facing the frog families.

"No choice," said Ronald, bluntly. "No, you do have a choice. Don't do anything different. Just stick your head in the shell again, and live with that guilt and feeling like you're the worst turtle this pond has ever seen. Or, you can let your guilt teach you something."

"Like what?"

"Like making amends. Your temper took over and you hurt some folks. Tell them how crummy you feel and figure out how to clean up the mess you made. Then see what happens to that guilt."

"But, I'm really scared!"

"Of what?" asked Ronald. "What's the worst thing that could happen? They make fun of you? They stay angry at you? They croak louder at night?"

"Yeah, all of that," replied Simon.

"Even if that did happen, how would you be feeling, knowing that you had done the right thing? Or would you rather live with that guilt forever?"

"No, nothing's worse than that."

"So," came Ronald's finale, *"time for a change!"*

*****

At the base of reluctance to change is fear: fear of the unknown, fear of failure, fear of disappointment, fear of being hurt. Rather than face and challenge the fear, we often back off and allow the fear to keep us stuck in our comfort zone.

When feelings are ignored or allowed to drive our decisions and indecisions without any message checks (Step Three), we lose our way and repeat our painful choices. The journey of change can terrify us, especially because it feels like aimless wandering. But remember, he who wanders is not always lost, particularly if he travels with his emotional Global Positioning System (GPS) to help him make choices that come from the best in him.

I recently had occasion to ask a client, "What kept you from throwing him out on his butt sooner?"

It wasn't time for insight. She had to keep herself safe from Carl, her ex-boyfriend, who was breaking into her home when she wasn't there. He wasn't physically abusive, as her former husband had been, but he was just as controlling mentally and emotionally.

"All these months you've let him rifle through your mail, go through your belongings, just to make sure you weren't doing anything he didn't know about. What happened to your boundaries?"

"I'm afraid," she answered. "Afraid to be with him, but even more afraid to be without him, or without someone. It's making me crazy! I was doing so much better, feeling stronger after we did that work on Steve, my ex. Carl told me that he would keep me safe from Steve. I was just afraid to be alone and unprotected. I didn't realize Carl would be just as bad, only in a different way."

The unchartered territory for this client is literally "no-man" land. She had never been without a male partner, and the thought of it raised all kinds of fears. She was afraid of being unprotected, but the very ones she counted on for protection were the problem. Her task at this point was to be clear about her fears, attend to them when based on reality (Carl breaking into her home), and then act (changing locks, enlisting police help, etc).

But the fears of being alone also need to be challenged. They have driven her into bad choices in her relationships. Being alone will be a different, hard, and major change. But loneliness won't kill her. An out of control ex-partner just might.

Often our struggles with change are not that dramatic, but they still create an internal war. I want to change. I don't want to change. I want a better job. I don't want to leave the security of this one. My marriage is miserable, but it's what I'm used to. I hate to see my child unhappy, but if I don't set boundaries, he will never grow up right. I was offended by a friend and am angry about it…but if I say anything to her, I'll lose the friendship.

Let's be clear: most of us don't like change. Even our unconscious doesn't like it! That's why it often attracts us to what is familiar, even when it's unhealthy. But change we must, or else resign ourselves to an unhappy and restricted life. It is our emotions that will help us through.

Our feelings are the signals that let us know what we truly want and need. If we are unhappy in a marriage or relationship, that feeling is motivating us to bring about a change in order to improve things or leave them.

The same is true of jobs, careers, and all sorts of daily choices for ourselves. *We fear making changes that will break our accustomed patterns and fly in the face of what others expect of us. And we fear what is unknown or unpredictable.* Fear will rule our lives until we challenge the messages that it brings (Step Three) and find the courage to live forward.

Fear, however, is not the only emotional player in this game of change. Anger, resentment, anxiety, excitement, guilt, shame, and embarrassment all enter the stage of life choices. When we change, we are often breaking a system of expectations, and even if we're okay with our choice, our relationships may not be. This is not unlike the change of leaving home physically for the first time. Or not returning home for the holidays for the first time.

One of our daughters has just faced this dilemma: to spend Thanksgiving with her boyfriend and attend the wedding of the person who introduced them to each other, or be with her family as she and her siblings have always done. Feelings? Excitement at traveling to a spa for the wedding with her boyfriend. Guilt for not being with the family.

Both are to be expected. With regard to the guilt, she had to ask herself (Step Three) if she is violating us. The answer is clearly no, because unintended disappointing is not the same as violating. But in certain families prone to guilt and guilting, the reaction to her not coming home might be: "Us hurt? Her *only* parents, who love her, would never, want her to be unhappy, don't ever want her to feel badly about *not coming home for the first time EVER in our family history!* Do what you have to do--we're only your (*sniff*....) parents."

If her mother and I had tried to guilt her in such a manner, it would have been even more important for her to ask whether she was really violating us. Once she realized that there had been no violation, then the guilt could be let go of as a false alarm. This, however, often leaves room for another feeling to arise: grief.

Recall the process of layering. Often we get stuck on guilt or anger when changing patterns, so as not to have to deal with the grief beneath them. Grief and sadness have to do with loss, and in not coming home for a holiday, we must face the existential (meaning, no blame) reality that things change, that we can't have it both ways all the time, that every choice is a sacrifice.

Often at the heart of reluctance to change is the fear of emotional pain. More precisely, the fear that we *won't be able to handle it.* This is where the courage to feel enters. As a society, we tend to be pain phobic. On an emotional level, we often don't want to deal with the pain either because we don't think we are able to, or because the pain may be asking us to address something or someone we'd rather avoid. We take pills to avoid pain of any kind. Yet pain is a messenger to be listened to, the harbinger of a deeper message.

Pain, in a word, has a purpose. Pain, however, that continues because we're repeating the same ineffectual behavior is pain *without* a purpose. This is my definition of suffering. A simple example might clarify.

Helen was experiencing repeated headaches. She took aspirin, but nothing helped. The pain repeated over and over.

"I don't know what to do." she complained.

"What's going on in your life?" I asked.

"Well, my marriage is sort of boring. I hate my job, and have for a long time. Every day I dread going into work. I'm not exercising anymore. I miss it, but just don't feel like going to the gym. And I'm still angry at my parents for disappearing over the holidays to some island. They never even sent my kids a Christmas card. Pisses me off!"

"Sounds like you may need some housecleaning and maybe a good dose of change," I suggested.

Emotional pain unattended will register in the body, telling us that what we're doing isn't working. We're doing the same thing over and over, expecting different results. It's time, as author Bill O'Hanlon would advise, to "do one thing different."

Four Basics in Mastering Change

1. **Consciously develop your own understanding of change.** It's not the enemy. It's an opportunity to grow, and it is *not* about being comfortable.

2. **Take responsibility for your life and happiness.** In other words, take charge of the need for change, rather than becoming a hostage to change and blaming change for your misery.

> **3. Develop the skills and knowledge base** to carry out the action called for. This very importantly includes emotional competence.
>
> **4. Specify and challenge your fears regarding change.**

Fear of change arises, understandably, at work. Job dissatisfaction can be a call for change, When one has done everything possible, including all the communication channels, in an effort to improve the work culture and has not achieved any success, the next question is: "Is this a place where I want to work?" If not, then I need to question the ultimate fear: "Can I/we make it if I lose my job?" That's a change that can be frightening in difficult economic times and when one is responsible to a family, given the possible outcome of job loss.

This is when we must listen to all of our feelings. Dissatisfaction will build, along with resentment, if there is no change. Yet, I must look realistically at whether leaving the job (the gain) would be worse than staying (the pain). Each person must answer this individually, but listening to all of the emotions and what they are pointing to is crucial in coming to some decision.

In any event, a game plan will be required. One plan would be to find ways of coping with a negative work environment in case one decides to stay. The other would be to create a plan of action if one were to leave. Above all else, whatever one decides to do, one must make it a choice, and not a powerless resignation.

Steps in Decision-Making

1. Listen to the emotional signals

2. Use clear thinking to balance those feelings

3. Make the decision

4. Create a plan of action, beginning with the first step, for getting to where you'd like to be.

And to avoid playing the victim (blaming, no sense of choice) in the face of change and decision-making, here are three questions that might help. Notice they all are about "I".

The Three Creative Questions

1. What do I want (listen to the emotional guidance)?

2. How do I contribute to the problem?

3. What do I need to do differently to bring about what I want?

Emotions and Addictions

Change means breaking patterns, and breaking any pattern is difficult. The longer the pattern exists, the more addictive it becomes and the less we can imagine ourselves without it. Eventually *we inaccurately think the pattern is part of who we are.* Our addiction to the behavior becomes part of our identity.

In many cases, addictions destroy lives, overwhelming the will power to act differently. Such is the case with drug and alcohol dependency. But an addiction, as I am using the term, can simply keep us stuck in the same pattern of behavior. We may not be drowning in waves of addictive helplessness, but we are still struggling for air. Patterns such as overworking, relational dependency, chronic blaming, and compulsive overeating fall into this category of addiction.

Approaches to breaking chemical and sexual addictions often begin with inpatient treatment in order to break the biochemical dependency. With or without such treatment, there is a need for strict, accountability-demanding programs, such as Alcoholics Anonymous (AA) or Narcotics Anonymous (NA). At times, medications are required to inhibit the biochemical need for the substance. But where do emotions fit in?

After the physical addiction has been controlled, the emotional work needs to begin. Typically, the urge to use an addictive substance comes when a feeling or experience seems too much to handle. This is precisely the moment the addict needs to attend to Steps One and Two.

Jolene drank when she felt overwhelmed. After years of addiction, losing jobs, depending on relatives to keep her off the streets, she entered a day-treatment program. She had stopped drinking, but began to imagine slipping out to a liquor store and purchasing a small bottle of vodka.

"So zero in on the moment, as if it were happening right now, that you first had that urge," I suggested in a session. "What do you notice in your body, feelings, thinking?

"You know, I've been living with my sister, who doesn't like my getting involved with George. She thinks he's a bad choice."

"And," I ask, "as you think of that, what's happening in your body?"

"This kind of churning in my stomach. Damn it, I can't keep both of them happy! Like I'm caught in the middle, the story of my life."

"And then?"

"I start to think about the vodka…"

Jolene had never learned to tolerate the anxiety and guilt that arise if she doesn't keep everyone happy. More importantly, she never challenged the false belief (Step Three) that it was her responsibility to keep everyone happy at all times. That drove her feelings. She lived from outside in, rather than from the inside (where she might discover what really fits for *her*) out.

The vodka (or drugs, or sex, or work) managed to numb and distract Jolene, so she didn't have to deal with her emotions that needed to be explored. Without the substance, she was faced with the impossibility of keeping everyone happy, yet never attending to her own authentic happiness.

An important question to ask when thinking about the use of an addictive substance or an addictive pattern of behavior, is *"What will I experience or feel if I don't use it?"*

Holidays were approaching not long after Daniel separated from his wife, and he was slipping back into depression, an old pattern for him. He was entertaining thoughts of cutting himself or mixing a cocktail of Tylenol and vodka.

"And I know I'm blaming, but if it weren't for her kids [his stepchildren], we would've been alright," he complained.

"So they were a part of it," I said.

"A big part!"

"And if you weren't blaming the kids right now, what would you be feeling?"

It didn't take him long to answer.

"That loneliness. The hurt, sadness. You know, Christmas and all…"

"And if you weren't distracted with thoughts of cutting or vodka, what would you have to hang out with?" I asked.

"Loneliness, hurt, sadness…"

Daniel's guidance system was reminding him, appropriately, that he had lost a good deal, and that his sadness and his loneliness were asking for attention. If he had continued to blame, or had cut or made that cocktail, the emotional pain would have simply stockpiled, breaking out occasionally in the form of blaming anger (displaced emotion) and more depression (muffled emotions).

Instead, he spent time in our session allowing his feelings and left a while later relieved. He agreed to ride the waves of sadness and loneliness if those feelings arose again. He had also learned the importance of bringing the feelings into contact with another human being. Burying our emotional responses and then isolating ourselves is a sure recipe for depression.

Change is hard. Changing ingrained and addictive habits is even harder. Yet full living is not about stasis; it is about growing and sailing forward. And each one of us has the guidance system to help us navigate the often choppy and changing waters of the journey we call life.

Chapter 18:

Born to Want: Empowerment and Emotional Honesty

"Follow your bliss!"

Joseph Campbell

The afternoon was warm and muggy. Without his shell, Simon had to seek out the shade of a large willow tree. Ronald tagged along, not ready to leave his new friend on his own. After all, a turtle without a shell in a huge wetland felt to him like a disaster looking for an opportunity. And even though he and Simon had been through a few lessons already, he had promised Simon's mother that he would look after her son.

Simon sat and leaned against the trunk of the tree, but his head began to droop almost immediately. Ronald was quick to notice.

"What's the matter, pal? You've been moping a lot lately."

"Dunno," answered Simon. "Something's just not right."

"Miss your shell?" asked the mouse.

"Still upset about all of that paint in the frog pond? It's nearly cleared up, you know."

"No, no, nothing like that," said Simon. "I just don't know. Just don't feel that excitement anymore."

It had been a while since Simon had left his shell and the tiny corner of the marshland that he called home. He had left with his drawing pencils and his new friend, Ronald, in search of beautiful things in the wetlands to draw. He had drawn a majestic willow tree, a butterfly, and an orange wildflower that hung like a lantern. That was all in the first day. Since then he hadn't drawn a thing.

"And I had a dream last night," said Simon. "Kind of scared me."

"About what?" asked Ronald.

"Well, I dreamed that my pencils were too big to pick up. Then my drawing pad was sort of greasy, and I couldn't draw on it. Then a huge wind came along, picked me up, and dropped me in a strange part of the swamp. No pencils, no pad, no shell."

"Might as well shoot yourself," quipped Ronald.

"It's not funny, really," said Simon.

"Sorry, sorry," answered Ronald. "But it's so, so bleak and hopeless. Do you ever get afraid that you made a mistake in leaving the shell?"

"Everyday," said Simon. "Like, I'm afraid to go on, but if I don't, then I'll never know, and I'll probably be sad forever from not having tried."

"Try what? Drawing? Leaving home?"

"They're the same thing to me," said Simon. "But I'm so scared that I won't make it as a swamp artist. And no home and all that dream stuff..."

Ronald folded his arms across his small body, a sign that he was about to hold forth.

"Want a suggestion?" he asked Simon.

"What?"

"Draw two things: a picture of yourself when you're afraid and one of yourself drawing yourself when you're afraid. See which one feels better..."

*****

I know two men, both artists, who struggle in their own ways to live what they love--creating art--so they can love what they are living. What makes it a struggle is the stark reality of economics. I had read about it and had seen it in movies, but here it was in front of me--two men struggling to live with integrity while trying to support themselves and their families. One was exploring drawing with crayons, the other, painting in the style of Rembrandt.

To imagine either of them abandoning their art out of fear was impossible. At one point, however, that was the case. They were not pursuing what they loved most. One would get filled with rage, the other would become depressed. At that point, their emotions were sending them different messages. One was reacting from a sense of violation and betrayal (rage), the other from a place of hopelessness and helplessness (depression). In both cases, their anger and depression became displaced, causing suffering to those closest to them.

The task they were neglecting was listening to *all* of their feelings. Fear was the first. It warned them that they might not make it economically. But they forgot to check out other possible feelings. They hadn't thought ahead to the emotional reactions that would come when they made their choices based solely on fear.

For a while, they forgot painting and their integrity. A life without integrity, without following one's bliss, is destined for rage, depression, anxiety, and addictions. The men began slipping into reactive anger and depression.

The three of us met for coffee one morning and began to tackle the complex problem of how to follow one's bliss without starving. It quickly became clear that the answer couldn't be an either/or, but had to be a both/and. I suggested that we each take turns answering one specific question over and over to discover what we wanted and in what order of importance. I related to them the first time I had been asked to do this.

A number of years back, I had attended a therapists' training weekend, where we engaged in an exercise to raise awareness of our deepest desires. The exercise went like this: pick a partner, sit facing each other, then one at a time, ask the other over and over, "What do you want?" Each time the question was asked of me, I found myself going to deeper and deeper desires and passions.

"What do you want?" I was asked.

"No more money concerns."

"What do you want?"

"Affluence."

"What do you want?"

"A red BMW convertible."

"What do you want?"

"A happy and satisfying marriage and family."

"What do you want?"

"The experience of no separation from my wife."

"What do you want?"

""No separation or distance from all people I meet."

"What do you want?"

"No fear.'

"What do you want?"

"Excitement about every day I live."

"What do you want?"

"No more fear of death….."

As I stayed with the same question, my awareness of wants and desires deepened. I learned that they all mattered, but some were more immediate needs than others. Some weren't even necessary (red BMW), while other, deeper needs required less immediate attention.

As we took turns asking each other the question at the coffee shop, my two friends and I realized that although some desires couldn't be met immediately, they must never be forgotten. These are the desires and callings, if you will, that make for our bliss.

Unhappiness often begins with the fear of following our own wanting, something we are born with to guide us in our journey in space, time, work, and relationships. Wanting, and the feelings that announce it, are the language of the Self. To deny them is to deny the Self's purpose for being in the world.

Dawna Markova describes this purpose beautifully:
I will not die an unlived life.

I will not live in fear
of falling or catching fire.
I choose to inhabit my days
to allow my living to open me,

To make me less afraid,
more accessible,
To loosen my heart
until it becomes a wing,
a torch, a promise.
I choose to risk my significance;
to live
So that which came to me as seed
Goes to the next as blossom
and that which came to me as blossom
Goes on as fruit.

In his book *Blink: The Power of Thinking without Thinking*, Malcolm Gladwell describes the process of intuitive knowing, the unconscious, instantaneous recognition as to whether something is okay or not, authentic or not, good for us or not. This knowing begins on an unconscious level and is conveyed to us by our emotional/body system. To ignore it is to ignore one of our most important ways of knowing. This applies to everything from what food does my body need at the moment, to whether I can trust or believe someone, to whether I should be in this relationship or not, and to what to do with my life.

This kind of knowing seems to come from someplace inside (that "inner voice" people speak of), where we truly know what is best for us. In terms of life vision, it answers the question, "What do I have a passion for, what makes my heart sing?" We know this instinctively and it is communicated through our feelings.

Of course, we need to check out the reality (or lack thereof) of the intuitive wants and desires. At times, our fears, biases, negative experiences or lack of information can cloud or totally derail this intuitive knowing. Mind and heart, conscious and unconscious need to collaborate. I would love to play one-on-one hoops with Michael Jordan, for example, but if I don't check out the reality of the want, then I need to decide where they will bury my mangled body.

In a word, this intuitive knowledge is gained by living from the inside out: living from an awareness of our authentic wants via our feelings (Step One), stepping into the energy of those feelings (Step Two), checking the emotional attraction to make sure that the want is coming from the larger Self, which is motivated by love, and not the small self, motivated by fear (Step Three), then letting the emotional energy motivate and mobilize us towards fulfillment of the want (Step Four).

In living that way, the place of control is internal, not external. Instead of making decisions for our lives based on what will please others, we begin by listening to our internal guidance system as to what fits best for us, and then moving into contact with the world around us. To ignore our Self-signals and to second-guess the needs and reactions of those around us is to become the yo-yo at the end of someone else's string.

Chris, for example, couldn't understand why his marriage wasn't getting better.

"I'm trying to be better, you know, doing the things Sarah wants me to do. But I'm never sure if it's what she wants or if I'm doing it right. She changes her mind so often."

"What happens when you don't do the right thing?" I asked.

"She blows up! Keeps on telling me I'm not trying hard enough. Says she wants me to be stronger and to do the things she asks."

Chris is living from the outside in. He tries to second-guess his wife, fails, she reacts, he retreats and tries harder to anticipate her needs. His anxiety then builds, as well as his resentment, which keeps him from functioning effectively in the marriage. And without her knowing it, Sarah's demands and intimidation create the opposite of what she wants. She gets a weak husband who orbits around her approval. Chris will have to push back and listen to himself more if he is to be the person both he and his wife want him to be.

PRACTICING A NEW WAY OF LIVING: *INSIDE OUT*

1. Be aware of moments of choice, whether choosing what to eat, which friendships to pursue, which job to apply for.

2. Listen for the emotional signals that tell you "YES" or "NO" (Step One).

3. Stay with the feeling without making any decision. What is it telling you to do or   not to do? If you find you're second-guessing yourself and wondering what the other person wants or thinks, return to your own feelings (Step Two).

> 4. **Check the motivation behind the attraction or repulsion. Is it fear? Love? Guilt? Excitement? Boredom? Resentment? Excitement *and* fear? (Step Three).**
>
> 5. **Allow the emotional energy to motivate and support you as you pursue what seems best for you (Step Four).**

Mythologist Joseph Campbell advised us to follow our bliss. This, like every act of integrity, demands the courage to express our uniqueness through how we live our lives. Above all else, it requires the courage to feel the signals that are emanating from the heart of our Being. There is only one of you, as they say. Only one authentic statement for you to make with your life, to give to the world, the ultimate Giveaway of the native American tradition. And this can only be accomplished when you muster up the courage to listen to what your wanting, expressed through emotional guidance, is calling you to be and do.

This wordless knowing played a significant part in how my wife and I made our choice about where we would live next. We had been living in a rural area of northern Pennsylvania for many years. One day, riding my bike along the Tioga River in the dusk of an early winter's afternoon, I came out of a wooded area and looked across the valley, to a region of greater cultural opportunities north of the state line. A feeling arose clearly--sadness, mixed with restlessness. I noticed it, and suddenly, in the *blink* of an eye, "heard" the words, "You're hiding under a bushel basket."

In that moment, I knew absolutely clearly that my wife and I needed to move elsewhere. It was time to bring what we had to offer to a larger venue, one where we could also find more cultural and social stimulation. I had had this thought many times previously, but now the emotional and intuitive knowing accompanied it. It was abundantly clear that the time was now.

Around this same time, as we questioned where to live, feelings of sadness and restlessness began to surface around my neglect of musical pursuits. In my late twenties and thirties, I was devoted to music. This passion fell by the wayside in the face of economic exigencies, a.k.a. potential poverty. From time to time, one event or another would inspire me to compose something, and so "The Long, Long Distance," a song celebrating a friend's wedding, recently came to be.

During one of my therapy training weekends, I brought this song with me. I had been training with this group ten years and had often wanted to muster up the courage to sing an original song for them. This circle of colleagues and friends had become my second family.

We sat in the room of a weathered Pennsylvania inn, fireplace crackling, and the moment to sing the song arrived. I could barely breathe. Something intense and unrelenting was stuck in my throat. So I sat still, seventeen other therapists wondering what I was going to do.

Awareness. Sitting with what was happening. Finally, sadness and fear took center stage, insisting on being attended to. Sadness that I had left music behind for so long, and fear that something so personal to me would be exposed and not accepted. Sadness took over for a while, then the fear, until I finally was able to strum the first few chords and utter the first words, "Love travels such a long, long distance, trying to find a home sweet home..."

"Sing it again, would you?" I was asked.

And so the muse found a voice after so many years of neglect. Whether it be in music, art, cooking, relationships, neglect the expression that your Self requires, and your emotional system will let you know.

The dreams we have when we sleep also bear with them emotional messages from the deeper Self, usually experienced as emotional "hangovers" upon awakening. Recently, I dreamed I had been invited to join a group of people who would gather occasionally to sing and play music together. Reluctantly, I accepted the invitation, and was listening to a woman singing a song of her own, when a butterfly floated into the room and, with its thin legs, somehow wrote the word "Hello!" on the wall. I awoke, feeling peaceful and full of the rightness of being with music, as if, in Rumi's words, I was being greeted from someplace beyond space and time.

Our needs and wants can also let us know that it is time to complete some unfinished business from the past. Allison had dreamed the same nightmare for decades. In it, a dark, male figure entered her room when she was an adolescent with the intention of sexually abusing her. She always awoke from the nightmare with terror and the fear of not being able to protect herself. We processed the nightmare, which paralleled an actual experience in her teen years, until it no longer bothered her to think of it.

A month later, Allison had the dream again.

"Damn!" I thought, "We took care of that! What did we miss?"

However, she went on to tell me that the dream was different this time.

"He enters the room, but this time I jump out of the bed, chase him from the room, and lock the door!"

She awoke from that dream with the feeling of strength and completion. After more than fifty years of a repeated nightmare and the fear-driven message that something was unfinished, Allison's emotional system relayed success through a sense of strength and contentment.

Whether awake or asleep, our deepest Self, our essential Being, communicates its desires to us in many ways, foremost through our feelings. If we don't listen to the emotional radar, we won't know what we want. If we don't know what we want, we'll get something else. If we don't know where we want to go, we'll probably wind up somewhere else.

Points of Attraction

In addition to guiding us and letting us know when we are on the path towards our own happiness, our thoughts and expectations, energized by our emotions, turn us into magnets, literally attracting to us what we are thinking, believing, and expecting.

What you focus upon, grows. Donald Trump expects to make a lot of money and looks forward to "the deal." So it happens. "I'm just not made to have good relationships," bemoans a client. That's what she gets. Spill a cup of coffee at breakfast, and exclaim, "This is going be one of those days!" And that's what will happen.

Recently Larry King hosted a panel of teachers and writers on the "Law of Attraction." Movies such as "What the Bleep Do We Know?" and "The Secret" show us that quantum physics is now verifying what spiritual masters have taught for centuries: we do, in fact, have much to do with the creation of our reality. Ernest Holmes and Wayne Dyer write about the same truth. We are not innocent and neutral bystanders to the happenings of our lives. Our thoughts and feelings are active forces of attraction for the people and events that appear on our doorsteps.

Why do wealthy people—many of whom don't seem to care much about ethics or humanitarianism—attract more and more wealth and the hard-working, paid-by-the-hour employees remain in their own economic status? The wealthy individuals expect the flow of abundance; the hourly workers operate by the laws that govern their perceptual box.

Then why is it that if I want blah, blah, blah, instead, I get quack, quack, quack? Because of my *emotional energy*. Affirmations alone are not enough to bring about changes. The positive thoughts must be charged with positive emotion.

If you want more financial security, but get the opposite, check to see where your emotions are concentrated. Most likely around the thoughts and fears of not having enough. If you want peace of mind, but allow your mind and heart to worry, your worries will begin to materialize. "I *knew* that would happen! It happens *all* the time!"

When we think about relationships, our emotional energy is often stuck in the painful experiences, the failures. We are emotionally focused upon what we don't want, and the magnetic power generated attracts more of the same.

"But I want an 'oh, wow' kind of guy, and I still get the quacks!" Loretta complained.

Some of her thoughts were about what she wanted, but much of her thinking and, especially, the feelings, revolved around what she was afraid of. So she got quack instead of 'oh, wow.' Intentionally or not, the emotional energy was on what she *didn't* want. So that's what she got.

In *Getting the Love You Want,"* psychologist Harville Hendrix speaks of the "imago", an unconscious template for relationships that is developed in childhood the way our primary caregivers related to each other and to us. This blueprint is charged with emotional energy, and, since the unconscious goes with what is familiar, it draws us to what we grew up with, *even if it's unhealthy.*

The task in relationships is to become aware of the unconscious, emotional magnet that exists inside us, and to consciously change our relational patterns by focusing on what we really want, not what we fear. We must entertain the feelings that support or go with those wants.

Our feelings indicate whether we are in alignment with our most authentic wants, energize us towards those goals, and are an integral part of the energetic field that attracts what we want. Without emotions feeding the vision of what we want, our unconscious system goes into a default drive, gravitates towards what we've been used to, and attracts it into our lives, healthy or not.

To honor our personal vision revealed in our wanting, to know the creative force of the alignment of our intentions and feelings, to employ that creative force, and to take responsibility for our lives is, simply put, empowerment.

Guidelines for Creating What You Want

1. Notice what the good feelings are attracting you to and what the negative feelings are warning you about. Check out the reality.

2. If what you are doing or the way you are being contradicts what you most authentically want, what is truly the best for you, then the emotional guidance system kicks in, typically with resentment, anger, guilt, boredom, ennui, depression, hopelessness. These feelings have been sent from your place of integrity. Time for change.

3. If what you want lines up with the best in you (happiness, joy, excitement), but for some reason is not allowed or feels like too much (guilt, fear, shame), check for injunctions, such as "It's selfish to want," "I don't deserve this," "I'm afraid I'll be disappointed," or, "I have to struggle." Add your own to this list and challenge them. They are simply false stories. Time to recognize them and leave them behind.

4. Recall specific times in your life when you've experienced contentment and peace. Did your thoughts (intentions), feelings, and actions line up?

> **5. Recall times of unhappiness, discontent, frustration. Did your thoughts, feelings, and actions line up then?**
>
> **6. Remember that wanting is the "voice" of the true Self when it is motivated by love, not fear.**

Empowerment rises from a life consciously chosen and courageously lived. This is freedom in its deepest sense. Not so much the freedom of choice to do anything I please, but that state of Being that is the fullest expression of who I am most deeply. This is freedom from self-imposed limitations due to fear and ignorance, the freedom from repeated and painful patterns, and the freedom *for* the bliss and the peace of living out our most authentic purpose.

This is deep integrity. Achieving it requires that we listen to and collaborate with our emotional guidance, ultimately discovering our authentic voice. Recently, I composed an alphapoem, one in which each line of the poem begins with the successive letters of a word, phrase or part of the alphabet.

ORIGINAL VOICE.

On any given day
Reactions from a very old story
Invade,
Grabbing and choking
Intimacy with my own soul,
Never
Allowing
Love nor light.

Victory
Only emerges
In the moment of
Courageous
Exit from the lie.

*****

Simon hung the two drawings from the lowest limb of the willow tree. When he focused on the picture of himself being afraid, he felt a twinge in his stomach. Then he became angry and sad, almost simultaneously. The scared face looked like he had felt all those years in the shell. He felt his throat tightening and found it hard to breathe.

He then stared at the image of himself drawing that first picture. Something lifted, energy began to move throughout his entire body. The excitement was returning! The image of himself drawing the scared face, and not just being it, set something free inside of him. He could step back, and be different. He was ready to do what he had set out to do when he first left his shell.

He smiled gratefully at Ronald and headed down the path to the edge of the pond, where his easel and a chorus of bullfrogs awaited him.

Chapter 19:

The Making of an Enemy: Emotions and Global Peace

"You know," said Simon, as he and Ronald watched the lily pads float on the clear pond water, "I finally had that conversation with the bullfrogs." He paused. "They thought that all turtles were temperamental and disrespectful."

"No surprise," replied Ronald. "No surprise at all."

Simon had kept his word, cleaning up the mess he had made of the pond water with a bunch of cattails. Then he had a heart-to-heart talk with several of the frog elders.

"But why no surprise?" asked Simon. "After all, I'm just one turtle, not all turtles. And I'm not even a very average turtle."

"Did they feel the same way after you had that talk with the elders?" asked Ronald.

"No, I guess talking changed it all. Before that, they didn't know me at all."

"Did you know much about them, other than their singing every evening?"

"That wasn't singing!" snapped Simon, but quickly caught himself.

"Maybe it wasn't singing to you, but to them, it's kind of what holds them together," said Ronald.

"Oh," replied Simon. "I didn't know..."

*****

I've been nonpolitical for most of my life. I am uneducated in matters of politics, both national and global. I try to follow the main streams of information, never knowing, however, what is true or false. What politicians promise and what the media reports have always seemed suspect.

Why, then, bring up the theme of politics in a book about emotions? The reason lies in what I call the making of an enemy. This occurs within and between families, between managers and employees, between ethnic groups, members of different social strata, between those who have and those who have not, and, ultimately, between nations.

Enemy-making is based on not knowing the other, on making a "you" into an "it." It is driven mostly by fear. Enemy-making begins by projecting our fears and assumptions onto others, especially those we don't really know, then acting as if our subsequent feelings are reality-based. This interpersonal pattern is of epidemic proportions. We view those who are different, darker or lighter, as immediately suspect. What we don't know might hurt us. So we project negative characteristics onto them. The stranger becomes the feared or suspected "other," the enemy.

Similar to cancer cells running rampant, these destructive interpersonal patterns spread rapidly, poisoning families, communities, and countries. They become intergenerational as well, promulgating genetic legacies of suspicion, hatred, and revenge. And the more we consciously or unconsciously place others who are different in an imaginary "internment camp," the more we feed a global propensity towards disconnect and, ultimately, war.

Grouping and generalizing about others is a major contributor to enemy-making. If someone offends or violates me, I need to be cautious around that person for good reason. If, however, that person is Catholic or Muslim and I begin to react to all Catholics or Muslims similarly, I have begun the process of projection in a big way. I tell myself a scary story. Worse, I forget that the story is my own creation, written on the unknown and nameless faces of an entire group.

Also contributing to enemy-making is another form of projection, in which I disown something about myself that I don't like, usually unconsciously. I then attribute it to someone else or onto a group. Author and meditation teacher Steven Levine relates a vision that came to him during a meditation. In the image, he was imprisoned in a Nazi camp, about to be sentenced by the Nazi commander. He saw himself as very different and much better than the Nazis. In the dream, he crawled to the booted feet of his Nazi judge, and upon looking up, was stunned to see his own face, unaccepting, hateful, and condemning.

The world suffers a great deal because we are not willing to face the prejudiced, the Nazi-like, the murderous, the deceitful, the unfaithful parts of our self. Carl Jung, the Swiss psychoanalyst, referred to these as the shadow aspects of our self, parts we must embrace and transform. Otherwise, they become stronger and more primitive, and are eventually projected onto others, creating us-against-them conflicts.

Self-awareness and emotional honesty can go a long way towards ending projections and stepping outside of protective identities (the tough guy, the rebel, the angry one, etc.). Whether I'm an individual or a country, if I can be the tough one, then I can get the upper hand. At very least, there's less chance of my getting hurt.

The downside, however, of such an approach to personal and international relationships is that my picture of the world becomes dark. If I have to be the tough guy, then I perceive others in a way that requires defense or attack. If I'm a hammer, then everything looks like a nail.

In this process, unfortunately, not only am I restricting myself with a limited identity, but I can't see the other as s/he is. There can be very little, if any, mutual understanding. How can we possibly know each other if we are firing at one another from behind masks and viewing each other through a distorted lens?

Finally, this strategy of strutting, posturing, and protecting keeps us from feeling what is truly happening inside. In hiding our fear, our insecurity, our shame behind these masks, we also hide the truth of who we are. In refusing to be vulnerable, we break authentic connection and become foreigners to one another.

Years ago, during the early days of our marriage, I used to become the irresponsible "other" in Barb's eyes when I returned home late from work. As long as she pointed her emotional finger at me, insisting that I was irresponsible, the more I fought back. As long as each of us was mostly invested in our position (turf battles), the war lasted.

It was only when Barb dug down into her feelings and realized that she felt unimportant when I came home late, that she took responsibility for her own hurt. As soon as she did that, I had no need to fight back. Her *perception* was that I didn't care about her, given her own history of not

234

feeling good about herself growing up. Her vulnerability and honesty ended her projection.

A classic form of projection and subsequent warfare goes by the name of assumed criticism. We all internalize to some extent a critical voice from childhood, usually derived from one or both parents. This internal monitor can become oppressive, so we project it onto someone else, preferably someone who actually is, to some extent, critical.

Gordie had grown up under the critical eye of his mother. His sensitivity to being criticized was enormous. He worked at a publishing house that went through reams of paper every day. His co-worker, Ruth, carrying her own fear of being irresponsible (instilled by *her* mother, a frugal immigrant from Lithuania), reminded Gordie to recycle the used paper.

Gordie had been trying to please Ruth in all sorts of ways, most likely as a way of preventing criticism. But he became furious at what he experienced as ungrateful criticism from Ruth. Rather than tell the truth about his own perceptions and reactions, he withdrew, convinced that it was Ruth's fault and that his silent anger was justified.

Ruth, experiencing his withdrawal, proceeded to do the same, assuming that Gordie was simply a petulant child who had never grown up. What Ruth didn't realize was the intensity of her "feedback," due to her fear of being irresponsible. And the war was on.

Projection makes enemies of individuals and family members. It also wreaks havoc when it takes place within larger numbers of people, ethnic groups or countries.

What happened to the Japanese Americans living in this country once Japan bombed Pearl Harbor? Internment camps. What has happened since 9/11 to many people of Middle-Eastern descent? Arrest and interrogation because of fearful assumptions and projections.

Can we even begin to conceive of the projections, the transgressions, and the fear-driven hatred that must be behind "ethnic cleansing"? It creates a false security, driven by a fear of difference, by a need to control that which is not meant to be controlled.

Fear, then, is a frequent motivator of projections and separation. It is often closely followed by rage and revenge, particularly when there has been violation and the experience of helplessness and shame. As long as each "side" insists on being right, on being the biggest, the strongest, battles and conflict will be inevitable. The emotional truth beneath the bravado, the name-calling, and the blaming remain unexplored, as does true understanding. Without understanding, there can be no compassion and no willingness to cooperate.

If it were part of corporate and international protocol, radical emotional honesty would go a long way towards preventing the dehumanizing of others. I am convinced that the courage of emotional honesty, plus an authentic desire to understand and be understood, can change the outcome of many disputes. Through conflict, community, rather than enemies, can arise.

If fears are clearly stated, rather than hidden behind guns, if shame is expressed and that expression seen as an act of courage, if rage and outrage are deeply heard, we might experience fewer wars. Would 9/11 have occurred, for example, if we Americans had been aware of the ways in which we have violated the rights and dignity of other ethnic groups through our national and corporate strategies? We don't know, but wonder we must.

It is unlikely, given the world in which they work, for corporate and international leaders to exhibit this kind of emotional integrity. The environment in which they operate typically does not permit such openness and honesty. For this reason it must come from, and exist between, individuals, families, and small groups. One person, one event at a time, with the courage of emotional honesty.

Chapter 20:

Sentinels: A Fantasy of Transgenerational Release

Ronald was talking about what Simon and the bullfrogs were learning from each other.

"So, they thought you were temperamental and disrespectful, right?"

"Yep, they were totally convinced," Simon answered.

"And you had no clue how important their evening croaking was to them, did you?"

"Nope."

"If that situation had continued, can you imagine what might have happened?"

"That's a very bad picture," replied Simon, after a few moments. "They probably would have made as much noise as possible, especially when I needed quiet. And I can see myself throwing more paint at them."

"And what do you think would happen if word of this spread around the swamp?"

"I'm afraid that a lot of frogs and turtles would start to take sides. They'd start to dislike each other even if they'd never met."

"Most likely," said Ronald. "More croaking, more shouting, more oil paint in the water all through the swamp."

"Like war," said Simon.

"Exactly."

*****

Traveling the hills of northern Pennsylvania and southern New York season after season, after snow, through rain into green, I am deeply moved by the guardian angels of the countryside. These are lone figures--a solitary tree in an open field, an abandoned shed sitting just beyond the edge of tilled rows of dry corn stalks, rolled bales of hay that sit silently.

They are the sentinels of my road trips. Their constancy and largeness always touches me, moves me to watch for them, photograph them, and leave a space in my heart for them. They emanate purpose that asks for no recognition. They seem to hold a distant promise.

I pass a poplar tree, erect, bare, limbs holding the whiteness of winter. In the middle of a cold, brown field, it carries the hope of a spring to come. Its dark outline, however, touches and awakens a story borne of part memory and part creative unconscious.

I slip into a dreamlike reverie. I am a warrior, native to this continent, keeping a wintry vigil at night, hunched inside a heavy buffalo skin, battling the seduction of sleep. As snow covers my shoulders with yet another blanket, I watch for any war parties that might attack while my tribe sleeps. The tribe elders and I both know that danger is close.

At some point deep in the night, all lies breathless. My head drops, awareness darkens, and sleep prevails.

Soon a cry shatters the peace and tears me from my sleep. A raid is taking place, and many of my people are being raped and slaughtered in their beds. "This cannot be happening!" I scream, jolted awake by the cries and smell of dying. But it has happened, and I must now bear the punishment of banishment from tribe, family, friends, from all that has been my life, for I have failed them beyond thought or word.

The images fade...Sentinels, like time passing, become a blur as I drive. The dream continues.

I know a warrior's insatiable rage. My guilt, shame, and sorrow are inconsolable. With a few who remain loyal to me, I turn my pain outward and indiscriminately seek a place to unleash the emotional storm. I undertake the path of the war god--killing, plundering, kidnapping, raping— whatever it takes to avenge what had been done to my heart and to all I thought myself to be.

I shift from the dream. It is still early morning, the countryside stretches awake, animals and owls rest from their nocturnal duties. I turn on the car radio and listen to NPR and the stories of killing and loss among the Israelis and the Palestinians the day before. I recall the image on the cover of this week's *Time* magazine: a Palestinian waving his bloodied hands at a frenzied crowd of countrymen after killing two Israeli soldiers. And in this moment I become aware of the powerful impulse towards revenge that still lingers from the dream.

Although images of that family and tribe being slaughtered still hang along the edges of my awareness, reinforced by the news broadcast heard just a few minutes ago, I stop myself from playing another movie of revenge in my head. Instead the images shift.

Again I imagine having lost those dearest to me to violence, but no longer as a Native American. In the theatre of my imagination, I now stand in the arid and barren space outside the building where the Israeli soldiers had been killed. I notice an elderly woman dressed in black, the mother of some enemy, standing in the middle of a bloodthirsty crowd. She cries for the loss of her husband, her sons, and daughters, her country. Her small, brittle body shudders, as do I, at the cold and frightening legacy between us.

I realize that this is a daydream. It's not real, yet it is painfully realistic. In ways large and small, I have lived all of these scenes, all of these images. This one, this old woman...it can't end the same way. Not again.

I return in my mind to the angry crowd and see myself stepping towards the woman cautiously. We slowly, tentatively approach one another. The crowd grows silent and watches.

We look into each other's eyes, knowing we have both lost so much at the hands of the same demon. Trembling from the deep loss we see in each other, we move closer, knowing that an embrace of acknowledgement and of forgiveness will quiet the convulsions of grief.

We stop, face to face. Our fingers touch, our arms open. Our hearts open as well, and grief becomes stronger than rage. In this moment of mutual holding, our tears release the waters of an old and sorrowful river.

And so the vision ends.

I continue to drive as the sun breaks through the night's watch. It does seem like a visitation, this woman in black, the warrior, and the solitary guardians of the terrain. The early light seems to bring clarity.

If we do not have the courage to be vulnerable and to be deeply wounded *with* each other, we will continue to make enemies *of* each other. If we do not hold one another in the midst of our most excruciating loss, we may well continue to murder each other with our unresolved grief and shame that seek another victim other than ourselves.

I drive on. Something in me wants to cry for the heartbreak of it all. I pray for us all to find the courage to stand together in our deepest grief. All of us, sentinels joined in the frozen places of our hearts.

Chapter 21:

Spiritual Bypass: Emotional Honesty and Spiritual Authenticity

In our sleep, pain which cannot forget falls drop by drop
upon the heart until, in our own despair, against our will,
comes wisdom through the awful grace of God.

Aeschylus

At times, Simon painted from the inside out. The shapes and colors on his canvas flowed from whatever he was feeling at the moment. They didn't resemble anything that lived in the swamp, but seemed to choose themselves. He did this best with his eyes closed.

Ronald passed by the painting pond, as they now called it, on one of those mornings when Simon sat with his eyes closed in front of his easel. He didn't move and wasn't touching his brushes. Ronald watched for a while before interrupting.

"Hey," he said softly, "are you okay?"

Simon was jolted out of his concentration.

"Oh, yeah, I'm alright. It's just that I can't get that feeling back, and I wanted so much to paint it."

"What feeling?" asked Ronald.

"Do you remember those mornings," Simon answered, "when we would sit by the spot where the water flows? Just next to that willow tree?"

"Yep," answered Ronald. "What about it?"

"And we would sit there, early in the morning just as the sun was coming up, and I just can't find the words for it. It was as if the water flowed right through us. And the light, oh, my, the light filled everything, too."

"Yeah," replied Ronald, "amazing moments, weren't they?"

"Right," said Simon. "But you know, when I still had all that guilt and stuff after I threw my paints into the pond, I couldn't feel the water or the light. Everything felt heavy and dark. I hated that."

"So things got worse before they got better?" asked Ronald.

"Yeah. At night, it seemed as if the frogs were all shouting nasty things at me. I just felt worse and worse."

"So what happened?"

"Well," replied Simon, "as soon as I cleaned up the pond and the guilt left, I felt this sort of lightness. And connected to the frogs and the pond. For the last few days, when I watch the water and the light, everything feels so close. Even more than before. It's so beautiful, all I do is start to cry!"

"Is that why you're sitting here right now?" asked Ronald.

"I'm just trying to paint that amazing feeling," said Simon. "I didn't have words to describe it, and now I don't have the colors."

"Well," said Ronald, thinking out loud, "it just may have to stay that way."

*****

In the ancient Greek play *Agamemnon*, Aeschylus describes the pain that leads to wisdom through the "awful grace of God." Robert F. Kennedy was fond of that passage, and quoted it to a large crowd of African Americans in Indianapolis, the day after the assassination of Martin Luther King. He reminded them that he, too, had lost a brother at the hands of a white man.

When we are facing our deepest and most painful emotions, we often stand at the threshold of the transpersonal. We are poised to pass through the thin veil that separates radical emotional honesty and authentic spiritual experience.

Clarifying Concepts

For those of you who are theistic in one form or another, when I use the words "spiritual" or "transpersonal," I am referring to a realm of experience in which we know ourselves, each other, and life itself directly, without the bias and limitations of space/time identities. A spiritual moment, in my experience, is one in which I know myself to be absolutely one with the source of all life and, consequently, one with all specific forms of life, namely, other people, animals, and nature.

For those who are atheistic or agnostic, think of "spiritual" as a moment or experience in which the absolute best in you breaks forth, a moment in which you experience a lightness and an open-heartedness that leave you feeling completely accepting of yourself and completely connected to others. Call it what you will, but these are what Abraham

Maslow referred to as "peak experiences." These are cracks in the dense wall of our daily routine that allow us passage into the more rarefied atmosphere of extra-ordinary living.

Elizabeth Lesser, co-founder of the Omega Institute and author of *"The Seeker's Guide"*, was recently engaged in a conversation with Oprah Winfrey on one of Oprah's daytime shows. To her way of thinking, "spiritual" has more to do with the yearning that is associated with the great questions of life, such as, "Who am I? Where am I going? What happens after I die?"

"Spiritual" is not to be equated with "religion" or "religious." Religions, in my point of view, are structures in which the original spiritual experiences that gave rise to the various religions are ritualized, providing the church members with the opportunity of revisiting the original experience. One might say, using Lesser's concept, that a religion's purpose is to satisfy the spiritual yearning.

The difficulty with the attempt to organize or codify any spiritual experience, however, is that the experience can become lost in a sea of do's and don'ts, rights and wrongs, us and them. Yet any religion that remains true to the original, unitive experience of the Divine can be a pathway to direct knowledge of that great mystery and, in so doing, remains spiritual. This great mystery is the unnameable source of all life, which cannot be conceptualized or even imagined. We are always approaching it, but, given human limitations, can never really get it, other than in moments of spontaneous experience, experience I would describe as spiritual.

Religion (from the Latin *re-* back, and *ligare* – to bind or fasten), I believe, serves its highest purpose when it reunites its members with a direct experience of the Divine. When it prepares one for and leads one to the edge of that experience and encourages a "leap of faith" into a personal encounter with God, the Divine, or life itself, it has entered with its members upon an authentic spiritual journey.

For the above reasons, I typically avoid using the word "God." I am more comfortable with *Life, Presence, the Great Mystery,* or *the Universe.* These are, for me, words that avoid the bias of traditional terminology, and, in turn, two slippery and dangerous paths. One path leads to the error of putting That Which Is Unknowable into a conceptual and restrictive box, which in turn gets in the way of true experience of the Great Mystery. The second path leads to the creation of more separation between each of us, and between ourselves and Life itself, which, at best, justifies a disconnect between people due to perceived difference, and, at worst, convinces some of the right to kill in the name of God.

Spirituality and Emotions

"Spiritual bypass" describes our attempts, often unconscious, to avoid emotional reality through our religious beliefs. It reminds me of the game of leapfrog we played as children, jumping over the hunched backs of other kids, to land at the head of the line. Spiritual bypassing is similar, in that we try to skip over the emotions we must move through. An example of this would be avoiding your feelings of anger at someone because that wouldn't be "loving your neighbor." This can never work, because it is truly impossible to get to "heaven" or any spiritual goal without being true to your emotions.

The good news is that emotional courage *can* be a way to transpersonal connection and spiritual experience. This entails going through that emotional fire to discover whatever lies on the other side, which is typically a place of spiritual unknowing, of indeterminate future. This can be uncomfortable and that is precisely why many choose not to take this step. The unknown scares the hell out of us. In spiritual traditions, this passage through difficult emotions has often been referred to as the dark night of the soul.

Yet, at the end of this journey is a place of freedom in the deepest sense. A place of being free from the false identities that cover our core Self with denigrating beliefs and stories. Here is transformation, moving from all that has restricted us, all of the emotions we have most feared, into peace and contentment that cannot be taken from us. It is the death/resurrection theme played out in our individual lives. It is the empty bowl of unlimited possibility.

The Greatest Projection of All

Projection, you'll remember, is an unconscious, defensive strategy that attributes to someone else feelings that really belongs to us. For example, I'm angry at you, but I'm uncomfortable with my own anger, so I begin to see you as the angry one.

In efforts to avoid feelings and experiences, a good number of my clients who believe in God or a transpersonal Reality, project their fears and self-criticism onto the deity, even though they proclaim that that Reality is Love. They imbue God with the characteristics of their parents. Effectively, they create God in their parents' image and likeness.

Toni, a committed Christian, was having a "dump on Toni" day.

"My kids don't listen to me, and Chip just doesn't want to spend time with me. And he was the one person I could go to for support. There's got to be something wrong with me!"

Toni had been convinced as a child that she wasn't worth much. Her father had once told her bluntly that he could never love her as much as her younger brother, who had been born with an autoimmune deficiency and needed more love than the other children.

I asked her, "What about God?" to remind her of her greatest resource. "Isn't His support there at all times, even now?"

"I'm not even good at being a Christian," she moaned. "I can't pray. I don't feel as if I deserve to be heard by God. I'm letting *Him* down, too. I'm just a screw-up at everything, even my relationship to God."

God had become, for Toni, a repeat of a father who judged, criticized, and saw her as not deserving love. She could never truly experience her God as long as she experienced him through the lens of her human experience and conditioning. She had to topple the false idol she had unknowingly created.

She did this by noticing the feelings (most likely shame, guilt) that arose when she thought of her relationship to God (Steps One and Two). She then had to challenge the messages (Step Three) that accompanied those feelings and contradicted her understanding of God as unconditional love. Specifically, she needed to challenge the belief that God was a critical deity, who was supportive and loving only if she was a good girl and suffered like her brother. Only then was she able to experience her God in a more direct and undistorted way, entering into a spiritual relationship that was based on love and not fear.

It is common, in my clinical work, to meet people from religious or spiritual traditions who are, at best, emotionally uneducated and, at times, emotionally phobic. Anger is often depicted as not spiritual or even sinful, particularly if angry feelings are confused with angry behaviors. But we have been created with--or evolved into, depending on your belief system--emotions for very good reasons. They are the signals that let us know if we are in right relationship with each other, our Self, and Life itself.

The concept of forgiveness, often misunderstood as acting as if an offense never happened, is one of those areas in which spiritual leapfrogging takes place, primarily to avoid the pain of feelings that are essential to the healing process.

Lucille had been in a car accident that permanently impaired her ability to walk, leaving her with chronic pain in her left hip and leg. The driver was a teenager who had been drinking, ran a stop sign, and plowed into Lucille's car. Many months after the crash, Lucille was still railing against the boy who destroyed her well-being.

"My pastor tells me I have to learn to forgive that little shit! I have to let go of my anger!" she bellowed. "Easier said than done. Every minute of every day I'm reminded of what that kid did to me."

Lucille agreed that she was paying a price by carrying around the anger, but to simply "let it go" wasn't an option for her. So we followed the feelings, rather than insist that she be done with them.

The first step was to acknowledge her anger and its rightful place in her response to the accident. When anger gets stuck, we have to look for what might be fueling it or what it might be protecting. The more awareness she brought to the anger, the more it slowly subsided, revealing a layer of deep grief beneath. Grief itself is often found in two layers. She hadn't mourned the loss of what her life had been *and* of what she had hoped it would be. Grief embraces both past and future.

Bypassing anger and grief, leaping over them in the name of the spiritual ideal of forgiveness, is avoidance. Until she allowed the anger its space and time, Lucille couldn't reach her profound sense of loss. And as long as her emotional system was blocked, there was no room for forgiveness, no place for love, and no hope for the return of happiness.

It's important to understand that forgiveness is not about liking someone or condoning his/her actions. Forgiveness occurs when I no longer hold the other responsible for my happiness. What happened to Lucille, unfortunately, did happen. It was what it was. Forgiveness really has little to do with the other person. It's not something we do for the other, but is a freedom we claim for ourselves.

Lucille's power resided in how she was going to respond. She could continue to feed the anger, creating her own misery, or she could explore awareness without judgment (acceptance) by feeling all her feelings and freeing herself from a prison of anger and fantasized revenge. It was a choice that could only begin with being present to all of her feelings.

Lucille eventually chose love. She raged, grieved, felt the fear of an unknown future, and finally found herself at peace. She was poised at the edge of new possibilities, no longer the victim. Her heart opened once again, not only to the teenager, but to her God as well. She had stepped into the state of forgiveness and was free to begin again. An anonymous author once wrote, "Never does a human soul appear so strong as when it foregoes revenge and dares to forgive any injury." This happens only with awareness of emotions first.

Another form of spiritual bypass occurs with people who are committed to a spiritual path, but are caught up with the external behaviors they associate with a spiritual life. The individual is more committed, often without knowing it, to the roles and identities associated with their spiritual path. For example, I must be calm, joyful, abundant, and positive at all times. Hurt, anger, sadness, or limited funds become a sign of spiritual failure.

A true spiritual path, I believe, uses every experience and every emotion as grist for the mill, as Ram Dass describes it in his book of that name. Whether we are dealing with the struggle to forgive or the seduction of appearances, there is only space for love and true peace after we have faced and released fear in all its forms, as well as false self-beliefs.

Emotions are never positive or negative. They simply are. Some are more enjoyable than others, but all serve the same purpose as radar. The so-called negative emotions give us the opportunity to clean house, correct our course, and continue the journey towards our spiritual or "peak" home.

The Dark Night and the Dawn

Spiritual authenticity requires emotional honesty. Spiritual openings may occur as the unexpected payoff for emotional courage, but only after moving through the dark night of intense and challenging emotions. Such "spiritual emergencies," as authors Stanislav and Christina Grof call them, can be frightening in their intensity, to the point of being misunderstood as breakdowns rather than breakthroughs.

Ronnie was a committed Christian who had been sexually abused as a child by both her father and her stepfather. Her mother, very dependent on having a male in her life, didn't believe her daughter when Ronnie told her of the abuse. Her shaming experiences, along with the modeling of her mother, set Ronnie up for repeat experiences in her adult relationships.

Ronnie was working on her memory of discovering that her first husband was living two lives. His job took him on the road much of the time, so it was easy to have a second partner in another state. When Ronnie discovered this, she confronted him and was met with angry denial. Her husband exploded, smacked her across the face, and left her sprawled on the bathroom floor. He never returned.

After a good deal of preparation, I suggested she start by remembering being on the bathroom floor. This was the bottom for her, a depth of helplessness and shame that she'd felt she could never crawl out of.

It was dark there, she described. Dark, with no way out. Abandoned, used, and discarded. And it was all her fault.

"I'm crying. Like I'm outside my body, and I don't think I ever want to be back in there again."

I waited. She continued.

"Okay, I can feel it now. God, so lost, so empty. I don't know if I can take this loneliness. It's so old, and it's always been there…"

"Just breathe, and see what happens next," I suggested.

"I just can't go on, can't get off the floor," she said. "Almost can't breathe…but I've got to. Got to…"

Time passed.

"Oh, it's so lonely in there. I hate this…and now, I feel like *I* did something wrong. Like I'm just a piece of trash. It doesn't make sense at all. *He* was the jerk!"

"Keep going, Ronnie," I said.

"And now it's just so sad. It's in my chest now. So tight there. But I just can't cry anymore…."

"Breathe," I reminded.

Ronnie was emerging. She was groping her way out of every feeling she had feared and avoided all her life by staying in devastating relationships. Taking the responsibility for her childhood neglect and her abuse was the price she paid for not having to feel what she felt at this moment.

"Oh, thank God, I can see me sitting up a bit off the floor. I'm leaning on one elbow…Now I'm sitting up straight. Breathing is easier."

"And what else do you notice?" I asked.

"It feels kind of sad, but just sad. Not all that other stuff, like before."

"Did the person you were *then* make it? Did she survive?" I asked.

"Wow, yeah! Of course…but she's making it now without so much baggage…like she's stepping inside of me now, but it just feels cleaner, lighter."

We paused, letting Ronnie soak in the new experience.

"You once told me," I said, "that you sort of knew you were a child of God, but you never really *felt* that way. How is that now?"

Ronnie paused. Tears filled her eyes, washing the lens darkened by abusive treatment and the stories about herself that she had taken on.

"I *am* a child of God. *I am!*"

More tears flowed, as she bathed in this new awareness. Being a child of God had been a concept. Now it was an experience. Now she was truly baptized.

The process of leaving that place of no hope was the journey of facing and feeling whatever emotions arose, making them conscious, and then challenging the false stories and beliefs that fed them. Ultimately, it was, for Ronnie, the journey out of the darkness of a false and painful self-image into the light of her true nature, the very Best that had always existed at the core of her being.

When we move through the dark night, it is not unusual to find it hard to recognize ourselves afterwards. This can occur after shedding beliefs and emotional baggage that have shaped the self-identity for a very long time. What the Grafs referred to as evolutionary crisis is a call to a challenge, and an opportunity. The more intense this process is, however, the more necessary it is to have the guidance of a professional to accompany us through the unfamiliar terrain. Otherwise we can become easily lost, overwhelmed, and confused by the experience.

Suzanne had been working hard to break her pattern of attracting abusive males. She ended her latest relationship with George, who then began to play emotional games by reminding her that he could break into her home any time he chose. Suzanne had taken every precaution to protect herself and her child, but was still anxious, even about situations that were perfectly safe. Then Suzanne had a dream, which I had her repeat and complete.

"I'm entering this sterile building," she began, "moving from one room to another, and every room is sterile and without windows. I don't really want to be here. Then I move into a very large room with large windows. As I move from one window to another, that damned George is outside looking in, trying to spook me."

"What happens next?" I ask.

"I just keep going. I'll outrun him, or something, but I've got to keep on. I'm really scared now, but I can't go back. I *won't* go back!

"Okay, okay," she continues, "now there's a door in front of me that goes out of the building. I don't want to run into George out there, but I've got to get out of this place. So I move towards the door, and I just *burst* out! Like I'm propelled... and now I'm standing in a beautiful spot in the woods. George is gone, the place is just beautiful. So natural and very, very safe."

"And what's it like to be there?" I ask.

"Oh, god, the anxiety is finally gone. There really *isn't* anything to fear. George is just a pathetic child, so adolescent. And this is the weirdest: I almost don't recognize myself. I've never been this way before. I'm actually not scared of being by myself, especially in this place. *Especially in this place.*"

In her sleep came the "awful grace of God." Suzanne was finally able to make the journey towards freedom from her fears and anxiety. In order to avoid these feelings in the past, she had entered relationships that presented the illusion of safety, but were actually re-enactments of her abusive history. Now she faced those emotions and the perceptions that triggered them, finding a safety that was internally generated. In the dream state, the best in her guided her through the fears and into a place where she hardly recognized herself. She could now experience herself comfortably and safely *without* a partner. The problem and the solution were inside all along.

We come into this world with emotions for very good reasons. To travel without them is an invitation to an unlived life. Honoring and attending to them assures us of the necessary guidance, not only through the hills and valleys of daily life, but towards the transpersonal, peak moments of existence as well.

Chapter 22:
Simon Says…

"It is only with the heart that one can truly see."
Antoine de Saint-Exupery

Simon and Ronald had traveled quite a distance. For Simon, it had been a journey of discovery as well as miles. He was so far from his old shell that he found it hard even to remember it. It was as if it had never existed.

In the time he had spent with Ronald, he had seen and experienced things that had once been unimaginable. The sunrises and sunsets he could see from his new vantage point were breathtaking. Some of the creatures he'd met in the marsh were exciting and some frightening: the beavers building their homes of sticks and branches, the wise owl observing everything below, the tiny fish that populated the waters, the curious fox that lurked at the edge of the marsh, the rabbits and birds constantly searching for things to nibble on, and, of course, his new, dear friends, the bullfrogs and their families.

The tall grasses, tiny flowers, and occasional tree were part of his world as never before. And the water never looked so beautiful, so graceful, and so necessary. It was as if the water kept everything going and brought life from one end of the marsh to the other. Simon was one happy turtle.

Things weren't always perfect, however. Being out of his shell, especially around that fox, still made him nervous, and rightly so. Lightning, thunder, and heavy rains felt much different without his shell. There were days when he worried about his next meal, and when Ronald was off on one of his projects, he simply felt alone.

He had learned to use his radar to find his way through the days and nights in the marsh. Actually, he was developing a bit of a swagger, not unlike the one that Ronald sported. He couldn't predict his future, but felt up to whatever it might bring.

Now the two friends were sitting on a fallen log, warmed by the sun.

"Why can't it always be this good?" Simon asked of his tiny, wise friend.

"It can, a lot of the time," replied Ronald. "But things change, and change isn't always easy, you know. Remember how hard it was to leave your shell?"

"Yeah. I hated that," said Simon.

"But you had to do it, didn't you?" asked Ronald.

"Yep."

"And looking back on it all, would you do it again?"

"Yep, again."

"If it was always this way, we might get bored. We might get stuck. If I hadn't changed, and if you hadn't, we never would have met each other. We wouldn't be sitting on this log together."

"But how have you changed? You always seem to have all the answers," said Simon.

"I didn't always live in this marsh," Ronald answered. *"I started out in an alley far away. Rough times there."*

"And...?" asked Simon.

"Ah, that's another story for another time."

Moments passed. To Simon, It felt as if something were shifting.

"So, will we always be together like this? You know, friends on a log?" Simon asked.

Ronald paused. His face clouded a bit.

"Not always, but a lot of the time, especially at times like birthdays, or your coming-out-of-the-shell anniversary. And times when you just need to talk," Ronald grinned. *"I feel excited when I think of a reunion, or a birthday, or that anniversary. They're sort of like the marsh water, coming and going."*

Simon was quiet for some time. At last, he let out a sigh.

"Yeah, I guess that's how it is," he said. *"Just like water."*

"You've learned to travel on your own. You've got your own radar working now, and don't always need mine to get you through," said Ronald. "So I'll come and go, but you'll always have what it takes to find your way."

Simon's dream returned. He saw himself traveling the marshlands, taking care of himself, making decisions, listening to his radar.

"I wonder if I'll come across some marsh critters that need to hear some of the things I've learned from you."

"Wouldn't surprise me," said Ronald. "Just pass it on. And maybe some day you'll have children, a family... Hey, you could teach them. *"*

This new picture took Simon's breath away. It was beyond anything he had ever dreamed. An entire family of turtles, a whole marshland, with a completely new legacy, a life outside the shell with the radar to make it happen.

"Oh, my!" he exclaimed. "The marsh would just be an unbelievable place then, wouldn't it?"

As they sat, it was as if a mantle were being passed from mouse to turtle. Both were deeply grateful, and both seemed to know that hope would endure.

*****

Brother David Steindl-Rast writes, "It is not love that begets gratitude, but gratitude that begets love." As I write these last sentences, I feel gratitude for each of you who has journeyed with me through this book. I hope that its content will go forth with you and serve you well.

We all yearn to be happy and to be well, to be whole and complete, and to be connected. Quenching this thirst requires a marriage of mind, emotion, body, and spirit. Believing in the possibility of such integrity keeps my spirits alive on a daily basis after listening to the morning news.

It is my hope that the stories I have shared--both my own and those of family and clients--have touched your heart, for it is in the heartland of our lives that we most truly see and most authentically connect. And as we do this, the web of human life expands and strengthens, and we return home, finally, for the first time. We are then most deeply free. Free, at last.

Endnotes

Chapter 1:
Williamson, Marianne. *Return to Love.*

Chapter 7:
Ford, Debbie. *The Dark Side of the Lightchasers.*
   An excellent book about projection.

Chapter 12:
Ueland, Brenda. *If You Want to Write*
Hendricks, Gay and Kathlyn. *Conscious Loving.*

Chapter 13:
In addition to *Conscious Loving,* good books about creating
relationships:
Gottman, John. *The Seven Principles for Making Marriage
Work*

Hendricks, Harville. *Getting the Love You Want*
Schnarch, David. *Passionate Marriage*
Welwood, John. *Journey of the Heart*

Chapter 16:
Bradshaw, John. *Healing the Shame That Binds You.*
    A classic about toxic shame.
Nathanson, Donald. *Shame and Pride*
Branden, Nathaniel. *The Six Pillars of Self-esteem*

Chapter 18:
Dyer, Wayne. *The Power of Intention.*
Hicks, Jerry and Esther. *Ask and It Is Given*

Chapter 21:
Books that touch on the interface of emotions and spirituality:
Greenspan, Miriam. *Healing Through the Dark Emotions*
Bennett-Goleman, Tara. *Emotional Alchemy.*
Kornfield, Jack. *A Path with Heart*

Other helpful books about emotions:
Damasio, Antonio. *Looking for Spinoza*
Dwoskin, Hale. *The Sedona Method*
Pert, Candace. *Molecules of Emotion.*

Andrew Seubert, LPC, NCC, is the co-founder of ClearPath Healing Arts Center in Corning, N.Y. A licensed psychotherapist for 25 years, he has an extensive background in Existential-Gestalt psychotherapy and in music therapy, and provides EMDR consultation and training for other clinicians. Andrew specializes in working with trauma, posttraumatic stress, eating disorders, and the integration of spirituality and psychotherapy. A passionate and engaging international presenter and workshop facilitator, Andrew lives with his wife, Barbara, in north central Pennsylvania, where they co-parented a blended family of five, and where he pursues his love of psychotherapy, music, writing, photography, fine cooking, basketball and racquetball.

For workshops and retreats based on *The Courage to Feel,* as well as other events, contact Andrew at:
Email: seuberta@mac.com
Web: www.clearpathhealingarts.com

Marc Rubin is a fine arts painter whose creative impulses extend from contemporary graphic design and a fascination with the intricacies of typography, to painting in oils in a tradition that is centuries old. His work can be seen in galleries throughout the Northeast, including Chestertown Gallery in Chestertown, MD, Lambertville Gallery of Fine Art in Lambertville, NJ, and the West End Gallery in Corning, NY. An award-winning designer and founder of Marc Rubin Associates, Marc works and lives with his family in Elmira, NY.

Marc can be contacted at:
Email: marcrubin@stny.rr.com
Web: www.marcrubinassociates.com

CPSIA information can be obtained at www.ICGtesting.com
Printed in the USA
LVOW01s0743200913

353253LV00008B/195/P

9 780741 447074